PIP

AND

LAMBY

Gabrielle Guo

This book was written under the guidance and tuition
of teachers at Primary Writers Education.
For more information,
please visit primarywriters.com.au

PRIMARY
W R I T E R S

Copyright © 2026 Gabrielle Guo
ISBN: 978-1-923601-16-1

Published by Vivid Publishing
A division of Fontaine Publishing Group
P.O. Box 948, Fremantle
Western Australia 6959
www.vividpublishing.com.au

A catalogue record for this
book is available from the
NATIONAL
LIBRARY National Library of Australia
OF AUSTRALIA

To my sister, Vivienne

Prologue

Lamby

"Flowers look good on you," Charlie mumbled thoughtfully as he placed a chain of daisies onto Lamby's furry head.

Lamby tilted his head up to see the daisy chain Charlie put on him. The blue sky pierced his eyes as he peered at his beloved friend, whose face was lit up with a smile. Lamby lifted his chin in pride and wore the flower chain like a crown. Getting up abruptly, he got a burst of energy and started chasing up and down the shimmering fields.

"Lamby! Stop!" Charlie chuckled and he brushed off the reeds of grass sprayed all over him.

Charlie patted the soft ground beside him, and at once Lamby settled down and sat down next to his owner. The hum of insects and the occasional sound of chirruping birds was all that was left to hear.

Lamby wanted this magical moment to last forever. But the sweet silence with his best friend suddenly shattered into pieces, and Lamby returned back to the dull, quiet present. His surroundings were also soundless, but in a gloomy, saddening way. As it turned out, he had just rewatched his old memory. He had rewatched a savoured clip from the day before. But it seemed so... *real*. He could feel that stiff grass beneath his paws, smell the bitter-sweet scent of fresh-cut grass and hear the noisy cockatoo that screamed every once in a while. Time seemed to stop all of a sudden when he and Charlie were together, allowing them to soak up their love. It seemed that all the pain, the loss and the suffering had left. In these moments of happiness, time was more fleeting but much more treasured. Lamby didn't hold onto the love and hope tight enough before he had left. Now it seemed as if he too had walked away from Lamby's life...

Chapter One

Lamby

Lamby tried wagging his tail when he heard a bell outside, but he could muster no energy. The bell - a harsh metallic squeal that announced human presence - seemed to be begging for Lamby to open the door. Could it be Charlie? He had left two nights ago and still hadn't returned. Lamby didn't know why or what he was doing. Nevertheless, he trusted that he would come back. All he remembered was him packing a few shovels and a… frying pan? Lamby had never seen Charlie cook, but perhaps he had adopted a new hobby.

Lamby ambled over to the door, avoiding the mess he had made whilst in his owner's absence and peered through the stained-glass window. Instead of his owner standing on the front porch, there was a fair looking lady dressed in a floral dress. You'd think that seeing another human would arouse Lamby, but instead, he bared his teeth and started to snarl aggressively. The lady scowled back at the unfriendly welcome, and her blue eyes skipped over and landed straight towards the tsunami of mess. Shocked, she decided to leave without another word.

Feeling neglected, Lamby's face fell when he realised that the lady wasn't planning on staying. Growling was his way of saying hello, but no one came aboard on that idea. He trudged back to the hallway, waiting for his owner to arrive home.

Perhaps… I could try to remember what Charlie said before he left?

Lamby paced back and forth, trying to pick up any clues on where his best friend had gone. *He said something about gold and Bathurst…? Where is that, anyway?'*

Perhaps going to Charlie's bedroom would help.

Lamby buried his snout into the piles of clothes and went digging through mountains of paperwork twice his size. He even looked under the dusty, unkempt bed.

But instead of finding a clue, Lamby just found a dead rat decaying in Charlie's empty wardrobe and a few cockroaches scurrying across the panelled floorboards. The room seemed more abandoned than it ought to be, giving Lamby a queasy feeling in his stomach. Charlie had only been gone for two days, and it looked as if no one had been inside for years now. The warm and lively bedroom that Lamby had been accustomed to was now an empty, cold and eerie space.

Lamby headed to the door when abruptly, he heard a hard crunch. He had stepped on something. He immediately lifted his paw and underneath was what seemed like any ordinary scrunched up piece of paper. It had lines of different colours and thickness traced all over it. Lamby's dark eyes doubled its size. Was it a picture...? No. It was probably one of Charlie's worksheets. Annoyed that he had allowed himself to feel hopeful, Lamby kicked the sheet away.

But then all of a sudden, he recognised a group of words - *Train System of Sydney*

It wasn't a drawing - but a map.

Perhaps it was a map of where Charlie disappeared to?

Lamby peered at the unruly map with the arrows shooting out in different directions and grunted in annoyance. How was he supposed to read with everything going on at the same time? Observing the different stops and colours, Lamby noticed a circle drawn around the word - *Parramatta*.

Wait - isn't Parramatta the town I live in? he thought, as he began to pick up the details and names written on the map. The more he read the map, the more he discovered. There were several annotations scribbled on, in thick, squiggly handwriting. One of them read, *Parramatta Station, catch the train to the Western Line...* And near the note, he found a word circled in bright green. Lamby could barely make out the town's name. *Bathurst,* it read in faded, bold italics. The words *Parramatta* and *Bathurst* were connected by one thick line. An arrow was drawn beside the word, and it wrote, *...Then ride train till Bathurst.* Scattered between them was a series of other routes. Bathurst was definitely where Charlie had gone.

Everything was building up now, brick by brick.

Lamby lounged beside the dusty, green sofa. The silence grew loud as his mind went on and on. Instead of napping, Lamby couldn't help but think of what he could do next in order to find his best friend. He kept on thinking and remembering the many happy memories he'd had with Charlie. He missed him dreadfully.

Charlie had only been gone for two days, but to Lamby, two days felt like two centuries.

Soon, Lamby started to drift off, renewing one of his last experiences with Charlie still there.

"Hey Beauie! Who's a good boy? Who's the sweetest, most brilliant doggie in the world? What am I gonna do without 'cha?" Charlie said in a squeaky voice. As soon as he talked like that, Lamby would immediately go wagging his tail to Charlie and let himself bathe in Charlie's showering love.

"Charlie! It's me! I'm the best doggie!" said Lamby, through a series of happy barks, and he would spin around in circles and do tricks.

Lamby loved it when Charlie called him Beauie. It was adorable, easy to understand, and it was the special name that only Charlie used. No one else knew about the nickname. It was a Charlie-and-Lamby thing.

An idea sprouted suddenly in Lamby's mind. It didn't seem ideal, but he had to do something rather than rot away, lonely and sad.

Lamby was going to visit the last place he had seen Charlie. He was going to Dalerei Plaza and hopefully find him.

Chapter Two

Pip

P ip, without a care in the world, had just returned home from school. He skipped into the house merrily, but skidded to an abrupt stop when he noticed Aunt Mandy. All the colour from her face had drained. Her face dropped in gloom as she lazed on the mangy recliner. Her dark eyes fell on a *Today Sydney* newspaper she was holding, but it didn't seem like she was reading - she just stared blankly at one article.

Pip dropped his leather school bag onto the wooden floor and slowly sauntered over to his Aunt, who was rooted to the chair.

"Aunty?"

As soon as she heard Pip, Mandy slammed down the folded newspaper beneath the armrests, hiding the page from her nephew as she let out a wheezed chuckle.

"What are you reading?" Pip asked, narrowing his eyes.

Sweat beaded on the side of Mandy's face as her eyes skimmed around, trying to find a foolproof answer. Before she could answer, Pip pointed at an exposed article peeking from the armchair cushions, which had a grainy photo of a young man smiling. Pip recognised him straight away, for they were brothers.

Pip's eyes lit up and he smiled. "It's Dennis! Why is he in the newspaper?"

Mandy breathed in sharply. She didn't want her nephew to know what had happened to his beloved brother.

"Uh," Mandy started, her stomach churning repulsively. Pip immediately sensed her nervousness.

"Is Dennis okay?" the small boy asked quietly, his eyes large in angst.

Mandy paused before letting out a loud, unexpected laugh, which made Pip jump slightly. "Of course, Pip!

Why wouldn't he be okay? They just discovered gold out at Bathurst. That's where Dennis went off to. Bathurst. Remember when we went there to see Grandad Ken? And we took a train?"

Pip nodded enthusiastically and beamed in delight. Mandy forced a smile through gritted teeth, not letting the truth slip out her mouth. She had lied. Dennis was *not* okay. But she couldn't have Pip know the heart-wrenching truth - if he couldn't even handle accidentally killing a bug, how could he know what was going on with Dennis?

After being shooed away, Pip went to the long front porch and sat on a rocking chair. He gazed out to the faint, blue sky, with a few wispy clouds lingering on the sides. Honestly, Pip never had a lot of friends. He was the opposite of popular - not hated, but not quite liked either. He was the measly teacher's pet, the goody-two-shoes, a social outcast who could still blend in with others. Often people told him to not be so uptight and be more loose and carefree.

Just as Pip was daydreaming, the door opened to Aunt Mandy standing at the entrance.

"Hey, bud, do you mind getting some of that rye bread from Wellington's? Thanks, Pip," she said, to which Pip nodded and turned to go back inside to grab his coat.

Dalerei Market was not far from where they lived - just a few blocks down. Pip rarely went *inside* the train station, but there were stores beside it, so he would always pass it while shopping for groceries. Little did Pip know, someone was going to come into his life and change it completely.

Chapter Three

———— ◆ ————

Lamby

L amby ventured around the block, hoping to find Dalerei Market. There were many signs pointing out directions and streets, but he couldn't read all the complex and fancy names. Many people passed him, looking at the small, unswerving russell terrier. But they soon looked away when he snapped his jaws at them.

After looking around for a little while, he saw a rather large sign with many words printed on it. He couldn't understand anything except for the words: Dalerei Market. Lamby's ears pricked up as his face melted into a softer expression. He walked towards the direction drawn onto the sign, and he was soon a face of determination again.

After a few minutes of staggering around the adjacent neighbourhoods, Lamby found himself at the arched entrance of the large, familiar market that he and Charlie often visited before he left. He knew exactly that he was in the right place.

Dalerei Market was an outdoor square located beside the cab stops and tall buildings. The area was decorated with advertisements and signs and there was a saddlery billboard installed on the side of an apartment that was rusty and falling apart. The square was very busy with people darting in and out everyday - businessmen working, housewives shopping for groceries, and children hanging out after school. It wasn't as bustling as it was last time Lamby was there.

Lamby was surprised at how people, especially children, came running towards him in awe. Compliments and eyes were thrown at him, and the small dog felt like a big magnet, drawing everyone in. This seemed like any dog's dream, to be showered in love. But instead, Lamby loathed this. He hated how much attention he received. It made him feel pressured and nervous. He only opened up to one human - Charlie - and that was it. Yes, a strange dog. He behaved a lot like a cat rather than a dog.

Lamby arched his back and stiffened up his fur, trying to look intimidating. But it was hard to achieve for a tiny, short-furred dog like him. Instead of looking dangerous and scary, children thought he looked fluffier and more "huggable".

But no one seemed to move closer, so Lamby returned back to normal. He was trying to retreat from the spotlight, when a shadow suddenly painted over him. Whipping his

17

head around, he came face to face with a little boy, his grubby little fingers prodding Lamby over his face.

The child lunged out to hug him, and Lamby jumped back in reply. He squirmed, wriggled and pushed, but the boy's fingers wrapped around him like glue. His grip was tight and strained, but then at one point Lamby found himself choking in the arms of the tiny devil. Suddenly, a deafening snarl ripped out of Lamby's mouth, and he found himself tense against the hard floor, a low growl rumbling inside of him. The boy flew back at once, his face painted a startled expression. His face was red and his chest was beating uncontrollably. He *definitely* got the idea that the dog didn't want a hug.

Right after Lamby had scared the boy, it seemed as if everyone in the square went quiet. Adding on top of the pause that seemed deafening, the boy soon exploded with tears. Unending streams dribbled down his glassy eyes as he ran to a lady in the distance who looked shocked. She was well groomed, and Lamby recognised her porcelain face straight away. She was the boy's mother, and the same woman Lamby had seen at the front porch earlier. The lady's perfect face fell and turned whiter than the marble pillars.

"Oh my word! My poor baby!" she bleated and immediately waddled over to her petrified son, who was still processing what had just happened.

After wiping her son's ruddy face with a silk plaid handkerchief, she switched from fear to anger in a heartbeat. The lady erupted like an overdue volcano vomiting out its lava-like feelings all at once. She whipped her head around and shot a glare over to Lamby, who was trembling in terror.

"Stay away from my son, you heartless creature," she snapped, before grabbing the boy's wrist and dragging him out of the square.

Lamby shrunk into a ball, embarrassed and frightened. He had never scared someone to the point of them breaking into tears. He didn't mean to. The growl just snapped out of him like a whip. But was scaring away a child worth making the whole square turn on him? Lamby didn't know, but he could feel the stares of the passersby burn holes through his back.

Slinking away from the unfriendly spotlight, Lamby returned to his original idea of looking for Charlie. Walking through the winding pillars, all the people seemed to be staring at Lamby, their faces wiped with fear and disgust. Many people must have seen what had happened. Running through a sea of legs, a loud, high-pitched noise whistled in the distance. He recognised the sound immediately.

In the background, behind a tall, speared fence, was a train yard. Beside the uneven platform was a dashing train, chugging and chooing, as smoke wisped out of the smokestack. There was a big mob of people gathering around, trying to get inside the train. Lamby wagged his tail and spun around, hoping to get a good look at the inside. He wriggled behind the gate through a small gap that was just big enough for him to fit through. He trotted around the platform, venturing around the train station. There was one big building that wrapped around the train track like a tunnel.

There were a few papers scattered across the cobblestone ground, and there were all sorts of things written on them. There was also a timetable of the trains and their routes. *Redfern to Newtown … 10:49 … Newtown to Ashfield … Ashfield to Parramatta … The Nearest Pub! … How to get to Kelso … How to get to Bathurst …*

Lamby squinted at the words. The headings were big and bold, but the text underneath was too small to read

- and even if the writing was big enough, the words were too faint.

Suddenly, a loud bell rang near the building which made Lamby jump. He scrambled around, trying to see what was going on. A train flew past, blowing a big gust of wind onto him. The train chattered and coughed and slowed down, soon halting completely. There were several people waiting to board, and Lamby could see through the small, tinted windows that there were many more people inside trying to get off.

Lamby scrambled around, then a thought ran through his mind. In order to get to Bathurst, he had to take the train to Parramatta Station. And there were two platforms in this station which meant one of the trains would be heading to the Western Line and the other would be the opposite direction. So there was a possibility that Charlie would be disembarking. Lamby's eyes lit up as he looked around hurriedly, trotting around trying to find a good view. He lifted his head to try and see amongst the blanket of heads, each one stern and dull. But there was no sign of a young, handsome man who was always gleaming. Lamby ran around the platform until he reached the end, and he had to walk back again.

Lamby walked around the station, examining each spot, as if Charlie would be hiding inside an old cleaner cupboard. Hours passed and there was still no luck. Lamby's eyes dropped, exhausted, his tongue sticking out in dread. He trudged out of the station and towards some shade beside it, which was full of people sheltering from the sun. He hoped that Charlie would be hiding there.

Sitting under the shade was a group of people, each carrying a suitcase, talking to a fair man wearing a dark suit. He held a notepad and seemed to be guiding the people to the right train according to their destination.

There was a hum of chatter and bliss in the air, but as soon as one man recognised Lamby as the biting dog from earlier, everyone stopped short in their steps and turned their attention to him. It hadn't even been a few minutes since Lamby arrived, and he was already well known by the plaza. And not in a good way. After realising that he wasn't fully welcome, Lamby turned to leave when one of the men in the crowd stood in front of him.

"I heard you were biting little kids, eh? Violence isn't allowed here, y'know," he said in a raspy voice as he crossed his arms, blocking Lamby's way.

Lamby didn't know what was going on, and he just stood there, looking back at the man. He seemed like any ordinary man wearing blue overalls until Lamby noticed a little badge hanging over his breast pocket. It read:

ANIMAL CONTROL DEPARTMENT

Chapter Four

Pip

P ip staggered over to the entrance of the plaza. People streamed in and out, running errands and holding mountains of groceries. This was the first time Pip had been to the plaza himself. He remembered when Grandad Ken had paid him a visit and took him shopping at the markets for the new souvenirs that were just shipped from Africa. Even though it was a work day, the markets were already packed with shoppers. The noise of chatter and laughter filled the warm air as the tiny boy weaved in and out of the crowd.

The winding cobblestone paths seemed to be unending, with each path going to a different shop. Pip stared at each stall in awe, admiring the colourful painted signs that advertised each business. He didn't even realise how much time he had used by simply browsing for unnecessary gifts until the big turret clock started its evening call. It sang in a ringing voice, reminding the townspeople that it was four o' clock, and that most of the baked goods and fresh produce stalls were soon going to close.

Pip didn't understand what it meant at first until he noticed the shopkeepers of a few stalls wiping their counters and pulling down the hanging tunics over their shops. Pip understood what was going on, but he still didn't know where the Wellington's bakery was, and he needed the rye bread for Aunt Mandy so she could prepare dinner.

The tiny boy shambled over to the closest person to him, who was a tall man dressed in a grey suit. Pip pulled onto the man's cuff, trying to get his attention.

"Sir?" Pip piped up, looking at the man with big, blinking eyes. "Can you tell me where Wellington's Bakery is?"

The man looked down onto his watch. It was fancy and embedded with tiny crystal-like gems.

"Sure. It closes soon but it's not far. Right at the end of the street, beside the fabric store. You have to cross a road," he said, bending slightly to match Pip's height. "It is beside the train station."

He pointed in a direction to which Pip nodded, before smiling and thanking the man. Immediately, he ran off, hoping that the store didn't close yet.

Pip exhaled as he looked around, making sure he was in the right place. There were many signs - perhaps too many - pointing to all sorts of places. But he found the bakery store quicker than he imagined because the train station right beside the store was distinctive and easy to spot. *Phew*. He had made it just in time. Pip placed a hand on the doorknob when someone suddenly jumped in front of him. More like… some*thing*.

Pip leaped back, startled, and rubbed his eyes continuously to make out what was in front of him, blocking his way. For a second he thought the nightmare from last night had come to life, but instead, it was a small, furry creature. The total opposite of a monster. It was a dog. He had his skinny tail tucked under his belly, and he fixed his big, dark eyes onto the boy.

Pip hadn't even processed what had just happened when a booming voice thundered behind him.

"Hey!"

Spinning around, Pip looked to see who had said that. Charging towards him was a big man wearing denim overalls. The clomping of his heavy boots could be heard from the other side of the market, and he didn't look like a person to mess with. He was red in the face and carrying a rather large net, swinging it around as he took each step. Pip soon found out that the man was chasing after the small dog that ran in front of him. The dog was shaking.

Pip didn't know what to do, and he kept switching his glance between the dog and the charging bull-like man. Pip looked down to the dog. It seemed as if their minds connected into one, and at once Pip could hear words. It was as if the dog were speaking to him.

Don't let him take me! I need to find Charlie.

Though Pip didn't know the dog, a sudden spark of energy lit up in them like they'd known each other for year, and they hadn't seen each other in a long time. The man stormed towards the dog, who winced in terror. But before he could get to him, Pip slid in front of the terrier, causing the man to skid to a halt. Even though Pip was an ant compared to him, it seemed that the man couldn't move with the small boy blocking his way.

"Excuse me," the man grunted, as he impatiently swayed the net, indicating for the boy to move. "I need to get to the dog. If you haven't heard, he bites people."

Pip looked down to the dog, whose big, truthful eyes told his story. *I did not! I swear. People just assume that.* The dog let out a few whines as he gazed pleadingly to Pip. Pip frowned before looking back at the man, who towered over them, tapping his foot. But Pip just looked blankly up at him and did not budge. The man grew impatient and grumbled.

"Boy, can you move please? I need to take him," he said.

Pip shook his head slightly, his pale eyes boring into the man's, as he said with ease, "That's not necessary, sir. He's with me, and I will make sure he doesn't wander off again."

The man cleared his throat and backed away, nodding sheepishly before waving a hand and leaving. After the man disappeared through the staring crowd, the two stared at the audience for a moment before Pip whipped out a small packet of biscuits and shovelled them into his mouth. He felt something prod at his leg, and he turned to see the dog nudging him for food. Saliva dripped from his open mouth, and his gaze latched onto the biscuits the boy held.

Pip understood at once that the dog was hungry. The dog was too clean to be a stray, but there was a glum look on his face that made him look sort of wild and sorrowful.

"You're hungry," Pip said, stating the obvious, to which the dog replied with a bark. "I'll get you some food."

Pip gestured for the dog to follow him, and it did, wagging its tail as it trailed behind. A shrill bell rang above Pip as he walked into the bakery, and inside was a plump lady taking out a tray of steaming cream buns.

"We're closed!" she cawed out, not looking at Pip.

"Please, missus, I'll be quick!" he said.

The lady placed the tray onto the wooden counter before letting out a sigh. "Alright. What can I do for you?"

Pip looked up to remember what his aunt wanted him to buy. "One loaf of rye bread, please. Thank you."

He handed over a sixpence to the lady. She placed the coin onto the counter and turned to prepare the order. Pip looked at the small desserts placed on the trays under the counter. They were fancy but small, each with icing looped on the sides. A decorated price sign hung on the counter which read *"Mignardise- small desserts for a sixpence!"* Pip was appalled at the price. Sixpence was a lot, and just for a small tart that couldn't even fill you? His gaze skidded across the trays when he noticed one bun with a sausage sticking out. Sort of like a hotdog, but smaller. *Two pennies.* The dog might like it.

"Uh, missus?" Pip said, and the lady turned around. "May I get one of the sausage buns?"

The lady peered at what the boy was pointing to before nodding and taking the last bun out and handing it to Pip. He immediately gave it to the dog, whose eyes were glued to it. As soon as Pip dropped the bun onto the floor, the dog started wolfing it down, practically inhaling it. Pip giggled and patted the munching dog, who didn't even show a sense of fear. He seemed comfortable with the boy, even though they met just then.

It was getting late, and Pip had just finished shopping.

"So, doggy, what's your name?" Pip asked.

The dog puffed up his chest, revealing a thin, leather collar with the word 'LAMBY' printed on it. The dog wagged his tail eagerly, as if saying, *"That's my name! What's yours?"*

Pip smiled. "Hi Lamby. I'm Pip. You're such a good doggy!"

Lamby's mouth stretched into a smile, and soon he started bouncing up and down beside Pip. For once he seemed alive again. Lamby licked Pip's face and the boy broke down in giggles. He didn't understand how this sweet, lovable dog would bite a child. The description just didn't seem to match. Pip bent over and stroked the dog's stubby fur as it bathed in his love. As he was rubbing Lamby's back, Pip looked up to the sky, which bled a mixture of crimson and purple. The sun was far behind the distant mountains, and it would definitely be over Pip's curfew, if he had one.

"Oh no," Pip said suddenly, and Lamby's ears pricked up. "It's late. Aunt Mandy must be scared."

The small dog looked thoughtfully to Pip until he abruptly got up, which made Lamby panic. Pip looked down to the confused dog and sighed.

"Sorry, Lamby," he started as he patted him one last time. "I need to get back home before it gets fully dark. But I'll find you tomorrow, okay? Meet me here again tomorrow morning, when the big clock strikes seven, okay?"

Lamby tilted his head. *Meet you here?*

Pip nodded. "Yes. Right here. Goodbye for now, Lamby!"

The dog was definitely taken aback, and he probably hoped in the back of his mind that the sweet boy would take him home. But he soon understood and looked down to the ground glumly. Pip managed a small smile and walked away slowly, surprised to see that the dog stayed at the same spot. He seemed very disciplined, and he didn't want to give a bad first impression to the boy. Pip knew it was going to be a long night for the both of them.

Chapter Five

Lamby

Lamby was really just minding his own business when the animal control man nearly started a riot with him. Soon enough, a wiry boy no bigger than him stood up for Lamby. He didn't know why he ran to the boy first. There was just a look to him that Lamby liked. There was something about him - those big olive eyes that signalled innocence and peace. It was like a sixth sense, and just like that, they had a connection. And just like he predicted, the small boy was the reason why he lived another day and was not sitting in the back of an animal control carriage.

Moments later, the two were sitting at the back of a corner store wolfing down some bread and sausages. But really, most people would probably feed a small, measly dog running about the streets. But not everyone would do the same to a runt who had a dirty history like Lamby. So he thought that the courtesy Pip showed was more than a good deed and that it meant something more. Every passerby gave him the cold shoulder and not a second look.

His name is Pip. He bought me food. He lied to keep me safe, and he could have just walked away like everyone else... but he didn't.

Lamby curled into a ball as he reviewed the last few minutes of his time with Pip, letting his thoughts catch up to him. There wasn't any time for him to overthink anything when the boy was with him. Lamby still couldn't really make up what Pip had really said.

Why did he leave again? Was it because Pip remembered that he had to buy something else? Or perhaps the mellow bell that rang was a reminder for all the children to go back home?

More questions popped up, and Lamby's mind churned around. Feelings, thoughts and concerns all spilled out. At least he was going to bed with a full stomach, and a small flame of hope that there was still kindness in humanity. The troubled thoughts of Charlie being missing faded for the night. Moments later, exhaustion got the best of him and flooded his buzzing head. Soon, Lamby was blacked out and lying on the hard, cold cobblestone ground of the square.

The first thing Lamby felt was the stinging sun shining through his eyelids. He burrowed his furry head, trying to black out the light, but it was no use - it was morning and time to wake up.

Soon, the commotion grew louder as people rolled in. Lamby stretched his front paws as he let out a yawn. Blinking, he looked around his surroundings and remembered that he had spent the night behind a bakery. Instead of smelling the usual cornmeal mush and oatmeal, there was a blend of fresh produce, pastries and soap in the icy air.

Lamby peeped his head out over a corner. Dalerei Square looked very different in the day. Slowly, he creeped out into the light. Suddenly, Lamby remembered everything that had happened the night before regarding Pip. He helped and fed him.

Where is he anyway? Oh yeah, he left. Oh wait! I think he said that he will come at seven!

Lamby ran his eyes over the square, eagerly looking for the tall clock tower. The distinctive tower quickly caught his eyes. *Six-fifty-one.* In nine minutes Pip will come and hopefully bring some food too. Though it wasn't at the peak of the day where customers were most common, there were already quite a lot of people and most of the shops had opened.

The dog paced back and forth, waiting for the boy to come. Suddenly, the sound of the bell started ringing. Lamby raced to see the time. It was exactly seven. He scanned the sea of legs, trying to find that one familiar face.

"Boo!"

A high-pitched voice squealed from behind. Lamby slightly jumped but quickly melted when he realised that it was Pip. He licked Pip's face, and he broke into endless giggles as he wiped his cheeks with his sleeve.

"Hi doggy. I'm back just like I said," he smiled. "Oh, and I brought you some food."

Pip dug through his small tote bag and retrieved a small stale bread. Lamby gently took the bun out of Pip's palm and ate it. Though he wasn't hungry, he still ate it.

"Do you have a home? An owner?" Pip asked, as the two sat on a park bench.

Lamby looked down. Pip frowned.

"Where are they?"

Lamby looked to the cab stop in the distance. "*I don't know. His name is Charlie Anderson. He left two nights ago. I think he went to the gold rush. In Bathurst.*"

Pip nodded slightly, then his face lit up when he realised. "Oh! My older brother Dennis also went there. My aunt told me that. He takes care of me and he's my best friend. So you don't have anyone to look after you?"

Lamby let out a small whine as he showed his big, dark eyes. "*I want to find Charlie. But I don't know how. He's also my best friend - and my only friend. People don't like me because I'm too loud and disruptive.*"

The boy patted Lamby, trying to comfort him. "It's okay, he'll come back soon! And tell you what, while he's gone, I'll take care of you. I won't be as good as Charlie, but I'll try."

Lamby couldn't believe someone would do that. He stared at Pip, a smile bubbling inside of him. Pip mostly just coddled him, but it was like they were talking at the same time. They rolled around in the grass, fed the pigeons and did simply nothing and just watched the clouds pass, and still had lots of fun. Even though Lamby didn't have a voice and couldn't speak out his feelings, he showed twice as much love than everyone else.

The two lay on the spiky grass in a nearby park and watched the distant trains pick up each group of passengers one by one when Lamby suddenly sat up and looked around. He lifted his black nose and sniffed the chilly air, picking up the nearby scents as Pip watched curiously.

Lamby continued to examine the variety of smells and odours while Pip's eyes scanned the park. His eyes fell onto the clock. He sucked his tongue. *Eight-twenty-nine.* Pip totally forgot about the time and he was late to school. He abruptly stood up and swung his leather bag around his shoulder.

"I'm late to school. I need to run before my aunt notices," he murmured.

Pip was preparing to leave when he saw a familiar figure in the corner of his eye - a lady, in a navy reefer coat carrying a bag of groceries. She seemed to be looking for someone. Pip's pale face fell, and he muttered something under his breath. He looked at Lamby and nudged him.

"That's my aunt. She must know I'm late for school."

Chapter Six

＊

Pip

Pip ran over to his aunt who was beside a lamppost. A concerned expression was painted on her face. She turned around and noticed Pip standing behind her.

"Sorry, Aunt Mandy. I totally forgot the time," Pip said sheepishly. He kicked a small stone under his foot.

Mandy stared at her nephew, deeply unsatisfied with the answer. Her face was red, and she looked more than exhausted.

"You forgot the time?" she started. "What do you mean, Pip? You never do this! The school messenger notified me all of a sudden when you left home for school! What are you doing here, anyway?"

Pip looked at the ground, not daring to look at his aunt's eyes. Mandy went through many emotions - upset, disappointed, confused and mad. But how did Pip even forget the time? It was such a foolish thing to do.

"Let's go now, or you'll be even more late to school. I hope I can trust you to go to school yourself. Behave, alright, Pip?" she said, and she led him out of the square.

The small boy walked on the edge of the road, still staring at the ground in shame. He had never done anything to make someone mad at him before. Even doing the smallest thing was considered rebellious for a saint like him.

As Pip strolled down the empty street, he heard a faint rustling from behind. He turned around. There was nothing. He kept walking, thinking it was just a small rodent. But the "rodent" turned out to actually be Lamby. He had followed Pip all the way down to his school gates.

"Lamby! Why are you here?" Pip sighed.

The small dog had a smug look on his face. Pip stopped in his tracks and waved his arm for Lamby to go back to the square, but Lamby stood still and stared back at Pip, acting like he didn't know what he was talking about. Pip grunted in frustration and he let Lamby follow him.

"Run along now, Lamby," Pip said, and he patted Lamby one last time. "I have to get to class. I'll meet you at the square again tomorrow and-"

He was abruptly interrupted by a booming voice calling from across the road. "Hey, nerd!"

Pip turned to see the people he least wanted to meet at that moment. He sighed and gave a glum look. There, standing across from him were three tall boys a little older than him. They were large in size, had a smug look on their rugged faces and seemed to have the same thought. Everything on them read criminal. The boys were late as usual and were known as the thugs, and they were a whole grade higher than Pip. They were known to pick on small children and targeted Pip especially, but they never really got to do anything bad to him since he was constantly by the teachers' sides. The boys were planning to get revenge on Pip after he snitched on them for cheating in a test. Now this was their chance - there were no teachers around.

"Who you talkin' to, nerd?" the middle one said, who seemed to be the "leader" of the trio. "Oh? Some weird stray you picked up on the street? Ohh, I get it now. You finally found your kind - clueless, lost and foolish."

Pip glared at him but didn't say anything. Lamby wondered what they were saying. He didn't realise that Pip was close to crying. He was a soft boy with a soft heart. One word would cause him to tear apart. But Pip just let the bullies torment him. The boys smirked at his blank face, and after a pause, they walked closer to Pip.

Lamby stood his ground, unflinching, but Pip wavered, slowly backing away. Lamby tasted the fear from him, but he was still unsure. His gaze flickered between the bullies and Pip. Once, he had been a fierce dog—unyielding, never sparing a second thought for strangers. To him, everyone was an enemy, and pity was a rare thought. But over time, he learned that not everyone was a threat. Gradually, that rough, unforgiving side softened, and he hardly judged others at first sight. So Lamby just stood there and waited for something to happen. *If the big boy takes any step closer, I'll plan what happens next.*

The middle boy completely ignored the dog standing in front of Pip and lunged into Pip's space. He swooped his huge arm in front and grabbed Pip by the collar of his shirt. Lamby's eyes flashed and he took up his space. His back became as stiff as a board as he locked his big, dilated eyes onto the bullies. A low growl rumbled behind his rigid teeth, and soon, a snarl ripped out. The small but menacing dog snapped his jaws as he barked, while letting out barks. Drool dribbled down his sharp jaws as he continued barking. The bully switched his glance to Lamby, all rigid and aggressive. At first he was anxious and didn't know whether to leave or stay, but after observing the dog for a while, the bully softened and realised that Lamby wasn't going to lunge out. Pip, on the other hand, was still in the bully's grip. Trembling, he opened his mouth to scream, but nothing came out.

"Shut it you mutt!" he hissed, swatting his big arm around, trying to swerve the noisy dog.

But Lamby kept barking. And he wasn't going to stop. Scared that all the noise was going to alert a nearby teacher, the bully tried his best to kick the dog away, but he missed every time. And before the boy could do any harm, a loud clang of metal screeched behind. Lamby quietened and everyone looked back.

A skinny man with square glasses and overalls was standing outside of the gates. It was a teacher, and he looked furious as well as exhausted. The boy immediately released his grip and threw Pip back onto the cold, cobblestone ground. The teacher walked over to the commotion.

"What's going on here? D'you boys know how big of a racket you are all making? Others are trying to learn while you three are late and disturbing everyone else," he spat, glaring at the three big boys, then looking at the small dog. "And why is there a dog here? Who's the owner?"

The three boys all looked to Pip, who was still speechless and petrified. He was obviously still shaken up by what had just happened. The teacher looked at the tiny, trembling boy and let out a weary sigh.

"Whatever," the teacher mumbled under his breath as he rubbed his forehead. "You three are late for the third time this week. I'm writing to your parents about this. I hope you weren't harassing other students again, Ben."

The boy in the centre nodded, flashing an innocent, toothy smile, knowing that his lies wouldn't slip out. "We were just playing, sir. Nothing else is going on."

The teacher frowned, unsatisfied, and signalled the bullies to leave. Ben let out a quiet grumble, and before he left, he gave a sharp glare to Pip that wrote danger.

"You better not snitch, nerd," Ben mouthed to Pip, who immediately knew what he had said.

Smirking, the three disappeared through the gates. After making sure that they had gone to class, the teacher looked down to Pip, whose eyes wandered off in thought.

"Were those boys bothering you again?" he said.

The answer was simple. *Yes.* They were bothering him. But the consequences of telling the simple truth could soon catch up to him. Pip was ready to spit out a flood of words that just unfolded in his mind, but the bully's warnings interrupted him. What would really happen if he "snitched"? But he didn't want to mess around and find out - even if it meant putting honesty last.

"No," he said bitterly, forcing the lie out.

The teacher frowned at him, unsatisfied, but nodded because he didn't want to disturb the peace. He was about to take Pip back to class when he realised that the small dog was still sitting aside, patiently waiting. He stared at the man, full of quiet expectation.

"Before I go to class, can I put him back?" Pip chimed, as he shifted towards Lamby.

The teacher nodded and waved a hand, signalling for him to be quick. He walked back through the school gates, trusting that Pip would head to class after.

Pip led Lamby to the back, slipping between the cold school walls and the long shed that stood beside it. The ground was blanketed with thick layers of leaves, their steps sinking softly into the rustling pile. They reached the door of the shack, and like usual, the rusted key was already stuck inside the keyhole. Pip twisted the key and swung open the door, revealing a dark and somewhat cluttered sight. The shack was used by the farmers and gardeners in the school, but ever since the Gold rush started, the gardens became wild and so did the shack. Lamby stared out into the what seemed never-ending darkness, both unsure and thoughtful. There seemed to be no lanterns or matches. Pip pulled down a tarp which hung above the side wall, and it revealed a small, warped window. Thin beams of light streaked through and the shack wasn't so dark anymore. Pip tried to unstick the window, struggling, and as it finally creaked open, he felt a fresh breeze once again.

"Okay," Pip huffed. "I can't send you back to Dalerei Plaza because I'm late for school. Can you stay here for a few hours? I promise I will come back after school finishes."

Lamby looked at Pip in thought. He didn't do anything. Pip paused and sighed, but the teacher was waiting for him. So he ruffled Lamby's head one last time, and he slipped out the door, leaving Lamby pondering.

Chapter Seven

◆

Lamby

*H*e was going to school. I followed him. Before Pip reached the gates, three big boys stopped us. They looked huge and much older than Pip. I didn't know who they were but Pip recognised them, and I tasted fear and anger. But there were mixed signals… I'm sure of it! I didn't know what to do. The boy in the centre grabbed Pip. He muttered harsh words that stabbed in my mind like nails. Some I didn't know the meaning of. Others I wished I didn't know the meaning. But before he could do anymore, a man came and said a few words which made the big boys leave. Pip seemed

shaken up, but he said nothing and put me in this shack and
disappeared into the school. Why would the big boys do that
to Pip? What did he do?

Lamby sat in the chilly shed. Only the faint sound of
the schoolchildren's laughter and chatter could be heard.
The shed door only opened a crack, but soon the wind
widened the slit until freedom was visible. Lamby's ears
pricked up as he padded towards the door. He popped
his head out, trying to see what was going on. Luckily, he
had a clear view of a small area in between two classrooms
where a couple of students would weave in and out once
in a while. But no Pip.

A shrill bell rang, and soon students started pouring out of
the small classrooms one by one. Lamby instantly sat up,
awake, from the loud commotion. He had fallen asleep
and for a second forgotten where he was or what he was
doing. But soon he realised that school was over and Pip
was now leaving. Without another thought, he darted out
the door and ran to the entrance of the school.

It was busier than Lamby expected. Dozens of students
streamed out of the gates, each one going a different

direction to the other. Lamby's head swelled. How was he going to find Pip in this big mob of people? He walked around, trying to find that familiar face. But then, he found someone he least wanted to meet. The big boy who Pip met in the morning was there with a crowd of students surrounding him. And in the center was Pip.

Lamby rushed over to get a better look at what was happening - the crowd seemed to be taunting Pip. He was at the edge of tears, his face all swelled up and dropped. The bully smirked and pointed, and said more sharp comments.

"What were you looking for?" he mocked. "Your mummy? She's *dead.*"

Pip breathed in and looked down in anger. The bully kept going, spitting rude gestures, mocks and insults.

"You have no parents. No one. You're so lonely you need a *stray* to walk you to school."

The bully suddenly noticed Lamby, and his expression shifted from spite to a smug, sarcastic smirk. The small, aroused crowd turned to each other and started whispering. The bully turned to face the small dog, who stood his ground, not looking away from the bully's eyes.

"What's this, Pip? Your little bodyguard? Is this mutt supposed to scare us?" he sneered.

Lamby continued his low growl. He couldn't understand what he was saying but he could understand the tone. The bully let out a laugh then turned to the jeering group.

Snorting, he picked up a small stone and started tossing it lightly in his hand. "What's it gonna do? *Bite* me?" He turned to the crowd for approval, raising the rock as if daring Lamby to react.

Lamby growl swelled louder, and his back tensed more. Soon the audience noticed his actions and backed off. The bully realised and scowled at them.

"It's just a dumb dog," he scoffed, and he pretended to practise his throws.

When the bully's back turned, Pip eyed Lamby tensely and mouthed the words, *'Let's go.'* The dog understood and snapped out of his rigid body. Before the bully could react, Pip swung his backpack over his shoulder and sped off with Lamby following at the back. After they left, no one said anymore jeers.

The two didn't stop until they were far away from the school, and soon all you could hear was the constant sound of frantic breathing and steps. The small buildings gave way to the quiet adjacent neighborhood beside Pip's home. Pip slowed down and stumbled to an abrupt stop, and Lamby skidded behind him. Pip sank to his knees and cupped his hands over his face. He had never ran so much before. After a pause of silence, he broke into tears. Lamby licked the tears off his cheeks while Pip clung onto him as he sobbed. The painful day had suddenly just crashed onto him.

[TEXT BREAK1]

"I'll be back, okay?" Pip assured, as he reached the front porch of his home. "Just wait out here. Then I'll take you to the plaza."

Then, he slipped inside, the door clicking shut behind him.

Chapter Eight

◆

Pip

"How was school?" Mandy called from behind the kitchen.

Pip dropped his bag onto the floor and collapsed onto the couch, not saying a word. He took a folded newspaper beside him and started flipping through the pages absently. Mandy turned off the dripping faucet and peeped her head out. There was something wrong.

She furrowed her brows and walked over to Pip, who was hunched behind the newspaper, covering his face.

"What's wrong? Did something happen at school?" Mandy said quietly, holding the paper down so she could see Pip's face. "School work? Teachers? Friends?"

The boy scoffed and rolled his eyes. "I have no friends, anyway." He shrugged and slid onto his side, gazing at a blank wall. "But it's nothing. Just grazed my knee, that's all."

Mandy frowned, but Pip just looked away, ignoring his aunt's eyes. Then, she started talking about school and how he should stand up for himself. She could be a yapper sometimes. Pip sighed and started to scan the room, pretending that the wallpaper was very interesting. He tried to block Mandy's questions as much as possible. He stared at the stained, olive green wallpaper, which was peeling off in one corner. He then looked to the small window beside the front door. The window pane was scratched with traces of bird poo still on it. *Ew*. But before Pip looked away, he noticed something furry through the window. He focused his eyes and remembered that Lamby was still waiting for him outside! After a moment of silence, he sat up and speed-walked over to the front door, still avoiding Mandy. But before he could lay his hand onto the doorknob, Mandy slid in front of him, blocking his way.

"Where are you going? You can't just leave without an explanation," she snapped.

"Dalerei Plaza," Pip answered, interrupting Aunt Mandy as if he was tired from all her talking. "I'll be back before you even notice."

Mandy didn't say anything, shocked at how her nephew was acting so differently. "Why? You're *always* going there. And you used to hate it when I asked you to go to Dalerei to buy some groceries! And why do you *volunteer* to go there now?"

"I never said I *hated* it. I just want to go there now to take my mind off things."

"Take your mind off what?" Mandy said, putting her hands on her hips. "You're seeing someone right? Something? It's that dog, isn't it? A teacher told me that you brought a dog to school and it created a lot of havoc while others were studying."

Pip's eyes widened and he looked at his aunt. "What...? He followed me to school! I can't just shoo him away! And I didn't bring him to school."

Mandy said nothing. "I'll be quick. I won't do anything wrong! Promise," Pip said quickly, and he slid behind his aunt and outside the house.

"Let's go."

Pip stormed out over Lamby, who was licking a rock at the side. He followed the mad little boy who started ranting about his aunt. Mandy watched the two out the window, quietly observing her nephew's actions. She unrolled the window and planted her ear into their conversation, trying to be unseen at the same time.

"...bullies. These days, you can't trust anyone! A friendly person is just too rare these days," she heard Pip say. "Trust no one."

Lamby looked up at Pip with big brown wandering eyes, and Pip let out a small chuckle. "Except for you, Lamby. You're my only friend, and you're all I will *ever* need."

Mandy understood the words much differently to how Pip had thought his words would come out as. Mandy's heart dropped. She frowned and looked down, a million thoughts racing by that sentence. *The only friend he needs? And that friend isn't even really considered as a friend?* It's a *dog*. Mandy didn't know what to think. Pip was a shy kid, but was he really this lonely? She kept listening.

"... yeah. Anyways, let's go now. You must be hungry!" Pip said, and Lamby wagged his tail eagerly.

The two started to move, and they were soon out of Mandy's sight. She sighed and looked around, unsure if she should chase after Pip or let him befriend strays instead of people. But she kept put for now and hoped for him to come back soon.

Meanwhile, Pip was walking further down the street with Lamby by his side.

"How much was the bread?" Pip muttered, patting his pocket for coins—only to feel it sag, empty. "Oh no. I forgot the money at home."

Pip frantically dug through all his pockets and groaned. He looked back to the direction of his home, and then back to Lanny. "I'll be back. You first go to the plaza, and I promise I'll meet you there."

Pip dashed off behind, racing back home. He passed the familiar bushes and then skidded to a stop, his breath heaving louder. He reached his front yard and stepped up, when a man dressed in a familiar suit came up behind him. He was holding a stack of newspapers.

"Are you the newspaper man? Yeah I live here, I can bring it in," Pip said.

The man flashed a small smile and gave Pip a newspaper roll and left. Pip tossed the newspaper in his hands as he entered the house.

In the corner, Mandy was still crouched against the window, hoping to find something. Pip frowned as he slowly approached Mandy. He was about to tap her on the shoulder when she noticed him and instantly straightened up, almost like Pip scared her.

"Oh Pip!" she huffed. "I didn't see you. When did you come back?"

Pip shrugged and stretched a hand out in front of him. "Just then. And by the way, do you have some money I can use?"

Mandy stared vacantly at Pip, still rehearing the words he said before. "Huh? What? Listen Pip…"

She slowly stood up and looked at Pip deeply. "I'm sorry, but I can't allow you to see that dog. You need real friends."

Pip scowled. "His name's *Lamby*. And he is a real friend. He cares about me and he encourages me. He doesn't care what I do or who I am… unlike the other kids in school."

"I understand, but you need friends who can actually talk to you and interact with you!" Mandy said quietly.

Pip pouted his lips and looked away. "He can talk! I mean, others can't hear him, but I can! Please, Aunty. And he needs food! A caring friend! People were so horrible to him before," he begged.

GABRIELLE GUO

Mandy hesitated and sighed, looking at Pip, whose eyes were glistening on the edge of tears. Then, she shook her head slightly. "I'm sorry. But I can't allow you to visit him. He's likely a dangerous stray that carries all sorts of diseases. He can find new friends, okay? How about this? I'll go find animal control and they'll go and visit him and find a safe home for them, okay? I promise they'll take care of him. Besides, he needs a real home, not a little boy who's juggling school work and taking care of him at the same time."

"No, not animal control! Anything but that."

"I'm sorry. I can't allow you. This is for your sake too," Mandy said sternly. It didn't look like she was going to change her mind.

Pip opened his mouth but nothing came out. He was in utter disbelief - so just like that, he couldn't see his friend anymore. He uttered broken words that didn't make sense. He felt the tears clog behind his eyes, but they wouldn't come out. He just couldn't believe it.

Instead of the whole world collapsing onto Pip all at once, it fell onto him bit by bit. As Pip ran to his room, he felt his surroundings blur. His breathing was ragged and hurt, and soon he could only hear himself.

Pip collapsed behind his bedroom door and crouched down into a ball. He wasn't really crying yet - he was still processing half of it. After a moment of staring at the blank bedroom wall, he looked down to his hand and realised that he was still holding the newspaper roll. He forgot to give it to Mandy.

The area where he was holding the newspaper was a bit scrunched, and he didn't even realise. Pip unrolled the newspaper and pressed down his hands to smooth it down. He wasn't fond of reading newspapers, unlike the other kids whose main talk was the latest news. But he didn't feel like doing anything else, so he decided to give it a read. The cover had a big photo of a new rocketing brand, but he didn't understand what it meant, so he flipped to the next page.

From Riches to Ruins? Australia's Economic Crash... New Land Discovered!... All Aboard Australia's Future Train System...

Pip scanned through the pages, trying to find something interesting that actually related to him. The words were so tiny that Pip could barely make out the sentences. He flipped vigorously through the newspaper, and after nearly going through the whole thing, he flipped to the last few pages and he saw the familiar words: *The Gold Rush - Latest News!* bolded in an inky black.

Pip's eyes lit up for a second and scanned the words. On one side there was a photo with two men smiling in the background each holding a tool, and on another there was a photo of a man holding an enormous piece of gold. He remembered Mandy telling him how Dennis went to the Gold rush, so that was something he related to.

Pip turned the page with quiet curiosity, his fingers tracing the worn edges of the paper. His eyes landed on a photograph, and for a moment, the world around him seemed to pause.

Dennis.

There he was—grinning, carefree, just as Pip remembered. A warmth spread through his chest, a flicker of nostalgia wrapping around him like a familiar embrace. Pip reached out, his fingertip grazing the image as if, somehow, he could feel his brother through the faded ink.

"Dennis," he murmured, his lips barely forming the name. A small, hopeful smile tugged at the corner of his mouth as he glanced down to read the title beneath the photo.

Then, he saw it.

The first word hit him like a hammer to the chest. His heart plummeted, an icy wave crashing through his body. The room around him warped—walls stretched sky-high, shadows creeping closer. The floor seemed to groan under his weight, as if ready to pull him under.

Pip's pulse drummed in his ears as he stared, unblinking, at the words before him.

DENNIS DUNCAN – MISSING

No.

His mind refused to accept it. His vision blurred. His brother—missing? It couldn't be. It *couldn't* be.

Yet the letters remained, cold and unyielding, giving Pip thoughts he never wished to have.

Chapter Nine

Lamby

Lamby sat in his usual spot, wandering. He looked abroad, hoping for Pip to meet him soon. He had been gone for a while now - was it supposed to take this long for him to get some money? But he remained patient and nestled down and slowly drifted into sleep.

"LAMBY!"

Jolting up, Lamby looked around, frantically trying to process what had happened. He was still half asleep, and it took some time for his vision to slowly blur back to life. In front of him was Pip, and he looked very impatient. He was wearing a coat, a small hat and carrying a leather bag. Sweat beaded on the sides of his forehead as he kneeled down in front of Lamby, staring down at him.

"We have to go. Now. Right now," he bleated, his voice cracking.

Lamby blinked and stood up. He was extremely puzzled. Pip gripped the still dog by the collar and gently yet insistently pulled him to move.

"Come on! Follow me - I'll tell you what's going on in a second," Pip said. He raised his speed, with Lamby trailing groggily at the back. "But I need you to follow close, alright?"

They passed many shops and stores until they reached the familiar, green fence. The two ran inside the train station. Pip looked around, the frown still painted on him. He dragged Lamby to a small stall, where a lady stood behind a wooden counter, helping a queue. She was talking to an old lady, who was showing her a small piece of paper. The lady was wearing overalls that the other staff at the station wore. When it was Pip's turn in the queue, he scrambled up behind the counter and peeked up. He was barely tall enough to reach the table. The lady looked down at Pip, a bit surprised and suspicious at the same time.

"How may I help you?" she said, bending over, trying to reach Pip's level.

There was a sense of rush written on his face, and the lady suspected it. "Can you tell me how to get to Bathurst? It's urgent, missus."

The lady slowly nodded, not taking her eyes off the measly dog who wasn't sitting upright. "Okay… Who's travelling with you?" She looked around, trying to find a slacking adult, and realised that Pip wasn't going to answer. She nodded and sighed. "Well, I'm afraid children under sixteen have to travel with an adult."

Pip's eyes squinted as he looked around. "I'm not travelling alone! Of course not. Who would think that?" He said abruptly, letting out a breathless wheeze. The lady raised an eyebrow, not buying a word. "Uh, she's not here at the moment."

"Oh yeah? Where is she?" she asked, half wanting to know what sort of tale the ditzy boy was making up.

Pip's tone shifted to a sorrowful, lingering tone. "She, um, has a sickness. It's called T-e-n-o-b-r-o-s-p-h-i-a Syndrome. It's where you turn slightly transparent and no one can see you until you touch some gold in Bathurst. Please, missus. She needs to get on the train before she vanishes for real!"

The lady's eyes twitched as she smiled impatiently, deciding to cut straight to the point. "I need you to get your story straight or you may leave. You are wasting my time and everyone else's too with your *sob story*. But since you don't have a guardian you *may not-*"

"I'm with him," came a honeyed voice behind.

Chapter Ten

◆

Pip

Pip turned around, dazed, remembering that he didn't have a sister. Standing behind him was a girl with chocolate hair and the lightest blue eyes. He exchanged puzzled looks with the girl who shot back the quickest glare that was barely noticeable. Pip stared at her, still pondering sheepishly. The clerk switched suspicious glances between the two. But coincidentally, the two did share several similar features which made the lady soften up a bit.

"Sorry, ma'am, my brother - and his dog - can be a bit… giddy sometimes. But I'm here," the strange girl exclaimed.

The clerk hid her agreement and flashed an innocent grin. "Nonsense, he's an angel" she said quietly as she examined the lady carefully. "May you give me your details, ma'am? And also your brother, too. And I'll secure you the next train right away."

The strange girl nodded and handed her a folded paper full of cursive writing and stamps as she recited her particulars. She smelled of a rich, cloying vanilla, that lingered around her like a thick layer of aura. "Barbara Mills, date of birth, September 18, 1853. I'm going on a train to Bathurst."

After a moment of silence, Pip realised that it was his turn now. He uttered and dug through his leather backpack for the paper. He had sneaked it earlier from Aunt Mandy's nightstand which was full of important things that he wasn't allowed to touch. He didn't really "steal" it - he just borrowed something that belonged to him. Pip's hands trembled as he gripped the passport tightly. He had never used the passport before by himself, and he remembered how much Dennis would rant about how important it is. If he lost it, did it mean he couldn't come back home? Would Dennis be angry with him?

Pip frowned. But that wouldn't even matter anyway since Dennis was missing. He needed to grow up in order to find his brother. After a moment of silence, Pip turned back to the clerk and slowly gave her the small nod.

"Perfect! Your form is all good. That will be thirteen shillings - Oh, twenty-six including your brother," the clerk said, to which the girl nodded and started digging in her small leather purse.

She scattered the coins onto the counter, and in return the lady gave her two, small papers, that were the train tickets. "Have a safe trip. And little boy, don't run off without your sister! Haha."

After Pip realised that the clerk was talking to him he replied with an unsure smile. The girl gave Pip his ticket and walked in front, expecting for him to follow him. Lamby looked at Barbara then to Pip, not fully understanding who and why this lady was talking to them. Pip stood his ground, and the lady walked further away. She stopped in her tracks after realising that the boy wasn't following her.

"Come on," she said, gesturing for Pip to follow.

Pip frowned. Was he really going to follow this random lady who lied to the clerk? Was he really going to go on a train alone with a potential kidnapper? Pip looked down at the ground then back to the lady, an uncertain expression painted on his face. He did have the ticket so he could just catch the train by himself. But then again, a little company couldn't be *that* bad. And perhaps she was familiar with Bathurst, so she could give him directions to the gold fields. She could also be heading there herself. Pip felt a gust of wind blow towards him. A train was entering the platform on the other side.

The lady turned around and her eyes widened for a second. "This is our train. Hurry, let's go!"

Pip nodded frantically and signalled for Lamby to stay close. He ran to the lady, following her up the planked stairs and onto the platform. A man in a suit emerged from the control room of the train, and he was holding a whistle. The lady grabbed onto Pip's wrist as she sped onto the train just in time. Pip felt the harsh wind whistle around him as he toppled onto the hard floor of the train. He turned to see Lamby already in the train, waiting for the two to settle down. Pip panted heavily as he wiped his sweaty forehead with the sleeve of his jacket. That was probably the most running he had done in his life. All of a sudden, a bell rang, and a man from outside closed the doors. Pip stumbled slightly when the train started moving.

The two silently walked down the long carpeted hallway, past the neighbouring compartments and rooms until they reached their accommodated cabin. The lady pulled the sliding door open and gestured for Pip to go inside. Still trying to catch his breath, Pip staggered to the nearest seat and flopped down, followed by Lamby who lay on the floor beside him. The lady perched on the seat towards him, being gentle and light, as if she was a feather falling to the ground. She tucked her pleated dress under her legs as she looked out of the window. After all that running, she still looked impeccable. Pip couldn't believe that she was only seventeen - she looked far more mature for her age - in a good way. The way her shimmering, chocolate locks were pinned into a pretty hairdo and the way she sat made her look like a young, posh lady.

The two sat in silence for a while until Pip spoke up, trying to get the story straight. "Missus, who are you?"

The lady just kept staring out to the passing surroundings. "I'm Barbara Mills."

Pip sucked in his stomach as he nodded with hesitation. "Okay. But why did you lie to get me on this train, Missus? And you also paid for my train ticket…You don't even know me."

The lady looked out absently, out the window, not looking at Pip's eyes. "Because I know your story is too important for you to miss the train."

Pip had a seed of thought. It made sense, he guessed. He mumbled before fiddling with his fingers, though his mind was still on the mysterious lady.

"But the tickets are expensive… and I'll just be another pain that you'll need to worry about, Missus."

"Then why did you get on? You had a choice to travel alone. It's alright, don't overthink it. Just think of me as your travel companion. Call me Barbara," Barbara assured. "So, what's your story?" She finally turned to look at Pip, her eyes soft and warm.

Pip paused. "I'm going to Bathurst. To the gold rush. I need to do something."

"Are you visiting a relative?"

Pip looked down and stopped fidgeting. He hesitated a while before answering quietly, "Yes, my brother. He went to the Gold rush before he…"

He stopped short, his words trailing off. Barbara looked at Pip and frowned, not sure what to say. "I'm sorry. I could never imagine."

"It's fine. He took care of me for my parents. But now he's missing, and I'm going to Bathurst to find him." Pip forced a wistful expression, smiling to hide his pain. Barbara gave a soft, empathetic smile and rubbed his back.

"So, you're travelling alone? Surely there's another relative that takes care of you?"

Pip looked up in thought, instantly remembering Aunt Mandy, who would soon be tearing the whole town down looking for her skittish nephew, never imagining that he was on a train to a town hundreds of miles away. But he was still angry about how she hid the truth from Pip. "My Aunt Mandy."

"Where is she?"

"At home. She doesn't know I'm here," Pip answered, smirking.

Barbara's eyes widened, and she stared at Pip for a few seconds, not clearly understanding what Pip had just told her. "What?! She doesn't know? She'll be tearing the house apart to find you missing! There's already one person missing in the family and she doesn't need another one! What am I to do…? I'm helping a ten-year-old kid run away from home to a place miles away from his home!"

Pip shrugged absently as if nothing had happened. "It's okay! I'll be fine. I know what I'm doing. Besides, I have all the help I need from my dog, Lamby."

Pip didn't know how long he slept for, but he knew that he slept enough.

He reluctantly flicked open his sore eyelids and he gazed out the window. The sky was a beautiful raw red, with thin strokes of scarlet and deep indigo spilling out from the horizon. The sun, hidden behind a mountain, created wispy streaks of pink and lavender. Soon the morning sun awoke from behind, casting long beams of sunlight onto the shimmering fields of grass. Pip exhaled quietly at the breathtaking view - he had never witnessed a sunrise like this before in the suburbs.

After a moment, Pip turned over to Barbara. Surprisingly, she was still sound asleep, a wooly sheet of blanket covering her. The air was damp and cool, and there was a bit of frost decorating the rims of the large window pane. There was a soft rumbling noise of the train chugging above the rails, the constant rise and fall lulling Pip to the edge of falling back to sleep again.

Barbara mumbled a bit, her eyes sewn tightly shut. Then the echoing noise of clumping footsteps came closer and closer. Pip looked back, trying to see outside his cabin when a hard knock came.

"Apologies for disturbing, but the train is soon to come to its final destination - Bathurst train station," said the booming voice.

Barbara slowly opened her eyes, mumbling as she shifted around uncomfortably. "Hm? What's the time?"

Pip uttered and looked down at his watch. "It's almost six. We're arriving at Bathurst soon," the man said.

Barbara frowned, her eyes barely open. "What man?"

All of a sudden, the train came to an abrupt stop and let out a shrill whistle, making both of them jump. Soon, the sound of chatter and faint footsteps came from the neighbouring rooms. Barbara yanked the blanket off and staggered around, frantically looking through the window. Outside was a station that looked just like the one in Parramatta. Barbara gasped and smoothed down her hair, stumbling to get up.

"We're here! We're here! C'mon, boy. Pack your things and let's go!" she cried, prancing around the tiny compartment, causing the floor to shake.

Lamby looked startled. He stretched his legs and let out a large yawn and got up quickly. Pip shoved his books and belongings into his backpack while Barbara put on her shoes quickly.

"Let's go, let's go! Yippee, we're here!"

As soon as Pip stepped off the train, the icy air blasted him in the face. He wrapped his woollen coat over his body, rubbing his hands in a circular motion, trying to heat his body up. Lamby followed behind him, looking around in amusement. Barbara walked around the station, observing the area carefully.

"I never asked," Pip started, as he caught up to Barbara. "But why did you come here? To Bathurst?"

"I'm visiting my father and my sisters. My father's in a hospital here and Margaret and Lola are on some holiday trip with their boyfriends," Barbara answered, her eyes lit up.

Pip nodded. "So you're wealthy?"

Barbara let out a chuckle and shook her head. "My father is, but not me. I live in a small town near Parramatta. Everyone else in the family lives in Hunters Hill."

Pip imagined how it was like to live in such an exotic, rich suburb - Hunters Hill. He examined the lady's clothes and accessories - big pearl earrings, a fancy designer coat with patterns threaded on it and a neat little bonnet.

She is definitely "rich rich", Pip thought.

Soon the two left the train station through the green gates and were off in a whole other town. As soon as they stepped out of the station, they were greeted with large grand buildings and clean roads and paths. Pip stared wide-eyed at the buildings and streets, while Barbara just looked like she saw rich streets like this everyday.

"Where are you planning to go now?" Barbara asked.

Then it hit him. Pip had no plan or idea of where he was going to go after he arrived at Bathurst. He guessed that he never thought that this faint idea would become reality. He looked around, unsure. "I don't know."

"Are you going to the gold fields?"

"Yeah. But I don't know how."

Barbara inhaled deeply, then she dug through her purse and took out a few gold coins and handed them to Pip.

Pip stared at her in disbelief. "No! I can't take them," he said, pushing the coins away. But before he could refuse anymore, Barbara shot them into his hands, making him stutter and give in.

"What do I do?" Pip half hoped that Barbara could stay with him a bit longer, or perhaps even better, take him in on his journey to find Dennis. Even though he had Lamby, a little extra company would be nice.

Barbara gestured to a group of men walking together in the distance, who were emerging from the train station. They were wearing thick attire and carried long bags and one was holding a pan. Pip watched them curiously, as Barbara squatted down beside him.

"You see those men? Ask them where the gold fields are. Or you can follow them. The fields are not too far from here. Probably a thirty-minute walk at most," she whispered, before standing up again.

After a moment of silence, a carriage with a few horses pulled up behind them, and a fair lady from inside peeped out from the curtained window. She had a porcelain face and wore bows, but behind all the makeup she shared similarities with Barbara. She called for her name, urging for Barbara to get inside the carriage. Pip frowned, concerned if this was going to be the end of their journey together. He looked up at Barbara with pleading eyes and bit his lip. Barbara looked down at him and sighed, crouching down in front of him.

"Alright, Pip. I'm afraid I have to go. But don't fret, we'll meet each other again. If you need anything, here's my address. Mail me sometime, will you?" Barbara smiled a sad smile and scribbled words onto a card. "You're a good boy, Pip. I hope you find what you're looking for."

Pip opened his mouth but only a faint utter came out. He felt tears welling up behind his eyes, but he forced them back. Barbara wrapped her arms around Pip and gave a warm, whole-hearted hug, for one last goodbye. Lamby cuddled around them too, whining as he sat beside Barbara. He didn't want her to leave so soon either. Pip could smell her usual scent of strong fragrance - though this would probably be the last time he'd ever smell it again. Pip didn't want to let go from the hug. To be honest, he really needed it. Even though he met Barbara just yesterday in the strangest greeting, she was like an older sister to him - and definitely not a stranger. It felt like they just reunited as siblings and now they were saying goodbye.

Pip forced himself to let go from the hug. Barbara climbed into the carriage. She peered out to Pip, who was on the verge of tears. So close yet so far away. Soon, the carriage rumbled, then coughed, and the horses in front took off slowly.

"Bye Pip! Good luck," she said, waving her hand out of the window.

"Bye, I love you, Barbara!" Pip called back, although the carriage was too far away for Barbara to hear anymore.

The cold wind blew onto Pip's rosy face, making him shudder. It had been ten minutes since Barbara left. But it felt longer.

It was now later in the morning, and several of the stalls and markets had opened. The townspeople weaved in and out of the fair buildings, holding bags of groceries. Pip passed a square full of food and entertainment, which had a resemblance to the one back at home - Dalerei Plaza. He had eventually caught up to the men holding the pots and pans walking in front of him, and their noisy chatter could be heard clearly. Perhaps their conversations might be helpful for Pip to find his way by himself.

"Aye, look mate, we're here."

"Seems like so."

"Let's go drop off our luggage at the miner's camp and get our rooms. Then we can go to the gold fields."

"Good idea."

Emerging from behind a large bush was a large piece of empty land of dirt and rubble. There were a few bushes here and there but most of the plains were bare and dry. Short poles surrounded the entrance of the gold fields, and a large tent was pitched at what seemed to be the entrance. Several men of all ages were walking around, carrying all sorts of tools. Dust filled the air, painting the sky a dirty grey. Pip observed the view in awe, watching a nearby man panning scattered dirt inside his pan. He didn't realise he was standing on the grubby road, until the rumbling sound of carts rolling and clopping of hooves echoed underneath. Pip jumped out of the way, barely keeping his nose from the carriage that sped past. On the opposite side of the road was a large building, which had a sign that read, *Bathurst Police Station*.

Pip ran across the road, with Lamby trailing behind, the two nearly causing an accident. He stared at the police station thoughtfully, before walking inside, hoping that they might have some information about his brother and Lamby's owner.

The foyer was large and spacious, with stretching walls painted in a dusty blue. There were signs and posters hung all across the walls, some that read certificates, others of the law. Pip scanned his eyes around, reading a few signs.

One read, *Animals Prohibited except for Service Animals.*
Pip bit his lip.

"You can't be here," he whispered to Lamby and
pointed to the notice, which made Lamby snort. "You
have to wait outside, 'cause we're in a Police Station!"

Lamby frowned at him in disbelief as if saying, *'As
if I'm going to tear down the walls and cause a mess like
an animal. But remember to ask them about Charlie!'*
Reluctantly, he trotted out the door.

In the centre of the room was a reception table, and a
man in uniform was standing behind it. He was scribbling
through a stack of forms that were scattered across the
wooden counter. Even though there was a chair, the
receptionist didn't sit down. Pip edged closer, and the
man noticed the tiny boy.

"Oh, 'ello, sonny. What can I do for you?" he said,
pushing away the papers and flashing a toothy grin.

Pip stammered, looking down. "Do you know someone
called Charlie Anderson? He went to the gold rush."

The man coughed and nodded slightly. He flipped
through the pages aggressively, nearly ripping the
corners. "Hmm. Oh. Yes. Charlie Anderson, date of
birth: January Seventeenth, 1841, Parramatta. His tent

number is thirteen. He was last heard from three days ago. Anything else?"

Pip smiled, relieved that Lamby didn't need to fear anymore. But he wasn't done yet. "Okay, thank you. Is there someone called Dennis? Dennis Duncan?"

Pip gripped onto the side of the counter tightly, sweat beading on the sides of his forehead as he stared hopefully at the documents, but his angle wasn't a good view. The man cleared his throat and skimmed his grey eyes across the papers. Then, he stopped short, and lifted one particular paper close to his narrowed eyes.

"Hm. Dennis Duncan. Date of birth: Third of April, 1843, Parramatta. His tent number was number twenty-eight…" he said, trailing off quietly, a frown painted on his pink face.

Pip instantly noticed the pause. He looked up, his eyes wide and brows furrowed. "What? What do you mean - *was*? *So where is he*?"

The man stuttered and folded the piece of paper slowly, before gazing down at Pip with sorrowful eyes. "I'm sorry, sonny. I don't think he made it."

Chapter Eleven

◆

Lamby

Lamby sat on the cobblestone ground outside the police station, loyal to Pip's orders. Even though once or twice a passerby would walk past him and comment a compliment at him, Lamby was still bored and waiting. He could hear the faint cawing of crows perching on the roof of the station and the clip-clopping of the horses' hooves against the road. He couldn't help the urge of going inside and listening to the news along with Pip. He didn't want to receive the updates from someone else.

Lamby squinted his eyes at the sun, which cast a warm glow. Near the gold fields was definitely not as peaceful as it was on the train to Bathurst. It was loud, dirty and hectic. Lamby was about to doze off when he noticed something furry and small scurry across the floor. The small rodent darted in zig-zags, jumping and prancing in Lamby's sight. Amused, he sprang up, barking in arouse. However, at the sight of the large animal in front of it, the mouse screeched and zipped through the cracks of the door to the police station. The dog bent low and sniffed the door's crevice, smelling the scents of human, paper and mouse. He barked, scratching the surface of the door. He nudged the edge of the door, managing to open it a crack wide enough for him to wriggle through.

Lamby huffed, examining the room closely, trying to find the mouse. He didn't even realise that he was inside the police station. *I'm going to catch you! Come out!* Lamby snapped his jaws, prowling low across the room when he noticed Pip in the corner of his eye, talking to a police officer. Immediately, Lamby forgot about the mouse and padded over to his friend. He panted and nudged Pip's hand with his nose. *What's going on?*

Pip's eyes were glassy and bright, and his muscles were tense like stone. He stared blankly at the police officer, who was looking down in grief. Lamby whimpered quietly, trying to get Pip's attention, except he was lost in disbelief at the moment.

"What...?" Pip whispered. "What do you mean... How did he...?"

The officer sighed and wiped his thick, bushy beard, reading a piece of paper. "The actual cause of his death is not certain yet, but on his way to the fields, he trailed off and... fell off a restricted area. It's confirmed that he died though. The news has just been sent out. I'm terribly sorry, sonny."

Pip cupped his hands over his gaping mouth. He didn't believe it. He didn't *want* to. "No way. No I can't believe that, I'm sorry."

But eventually, he'd need to believe it. He'd need to accept the truth even if it was painful and devastating. Pip couldn't hold it any longer. He felt the stinging sensation of hot tears building up inside. There was a burning throb in his eyes, and he felt like a spike crawling up his throat. After everything that had happened - everything Dennis had done for him... did it all mean nothing now?

Pip expected tears to rush out any moment. But they never came out.

Pip ran out the station, his face red and sweaty. Tears and snot blocked his throat, making him gasp and snort. Lamby ran after him. *Pip! Please. You have to listen to me. Dennis is not dead.*

Angry tears streamed down from Pip's glassy eyes. "He is. It's confirmed. We went all this way for nothing. I knew that I should've just stayed at home. I knew that Dennis shouldn't have gone to Bathurst in the first place."

You can't say that! He's not dead. Please believe me, we just have to find him -

"Hush, Lamby! Stop barking. You already heard it from the police, he's *dead*. We can't do anything except go back home.

Pip crouched onto the curb of the road and put his hands over his forehead, peering down in grief. Lamby walked over to him, approaching him slowly. *We can find him, Pip. Just trust me-*

"Lamby! Just stop lying. You heard it with your own ears, there's no use doubting the truth! It's just the way it is. I know, you're just trying to help, but at this point there's no use! Now scram!" Pip shrieked.

Lamby had never heard Pip raise his voice. Pip never remembered raising his voice before either. He just exploded out - like a firecracker bursting out in flames and spark. Lamby jumped back, flinching. The words felt like knives, shooting out of Pip's mouth and burning through Lamby's skin. There was no use in trying to help him anymore. He was in pain. Lamby couldn't imagine how it would feel if he lost his owner. He couldn't blame Pip for expressing his feelings, though he would have never thought someone so soft-hearted would say something like that. Pip needed space, and all that Lamby would do is more harm.

Lamby wandered around the busy streets, deciding to take a short stroll before returning back to Pip. The clamor of the market faded behind him - the clatter of pans in the gold fields, chattering voices, the clink of shop signs swaying in the breeze - all fading into a distant hum. Lamby crossed a patch of mud that squelched underneath his soft paws. He groaned in disgust and waded through the thick sludge and back to the clean ground. He padded against the ground, feeling the sudden change from smooth cobblestone to rigid, cracked pavement, as if something unsettling was leading ahead. The air was cool and brittle, with something lingering in the atmosphere. Lamby took a deep breath, breathing in the minty air when he reached an arched entryway. It was a graveyard.

Lamby felt the wind pull him into the gloomy cemetery, as if something was urging for him to go inside.

Just step. Just step through. Lamby slowly edged closer, soon entering through the archway. It seemed as if everything behind the arched entryway had instantly turned dull and gloomy. Lamby trudged along the slim, pebble trail, between several tombstones. Each one was like a snowflake - each with different shapes and sizes. One was a grey stone carved into a weeping angel. The angel was coiled into a ball, with her face peeping out from a side behind her large, thick wings. Though the stone was aged and crumbling, if you looked closely, you could see that there were tiny, stone lines seeping out of her begging eyes. The edge of the angel was round and bumpy, laced with a trace of moss and dirt. Tiny flowers blossomed out on the sides of the angel's face. Lamby observed the cold stone.

Beside the tombstone was another one, a large cross. There were a few flowers laid on the stone, but they were curled and wilted. Small patches of brown filled the soft, white petals. Time for new flowers, perhaps. There were tiny, gold plates embedded in the stones, but they were unkept and decomposing so that you could barely read the names on some.

Two of the tombstones were identical. They were an upright stone slab of granite, with the same daisy chain laced around it. There was a fresh bouquet of mixed flowers, neatly laced on the newly-cleaned base underneath the tombstones. The flowers seemed so fresh that they might have been placed not too long ago. Tiny drawings of hearts and a stick-figure family had been drawn on both.

Martha Joan Sterling - Born on July 24, 1798. Loving mother, wife and sister. Kind nurse that helped hundreds. Died of cancer, November, 29, 1865.

Johnathan June Sterling - Born on September 28, 1795. Affectionate father and husband. Worked as a talented carpenter. Died of age, March, 13, 1870.

Another tombstone was newer. Cleaner. It looked as if it was installed just about a week ago. Except, there were no flowers. Or drawings. Or daisy chains. Just a slab with a small gold plate at the bottom. Lamby shifted to see the plaque. But it seemed hard for him to keep reading after seeing the name of the tombstone that it belonged to. He felt his throat tighten and close up. His mouth became dry and bitter, and soon he couldn't breathe. Lamby's eyes blurred, fixated on the tiny, shimmering plaque. He bent low and sniffed it. The stench of fresh metal reeked the area. He could taste it in his mouth. Lamby squeezed his eyes shut before reading the plate again, hoping that it was just his mind playing tricks. But no. The same words were imprinted on the plaque, not disappearing. Lamby's worst nightmare had become reality.

Charlie Anderson - died in the Gold Rush, 1874.

There was no other information about Charlie's death. That was all it said. No specific date, no reason. Could it be another Charlie Anderson? But even if it was, something in Lamby's chest tightened like he already knew the truth. Lamby always thought of the sunny side of things. Even on the worst days. But right now, it felt like there was no point anymore. In anything. Lamby felt hot, fat tears blocking his eyes. His vision became shiny and blurred. How did he find out just now? A young lady walked right up to Lamby. Or the tombstone. She had a black dress and wore a black hat. A veil covered half of her pale, oval face, and when she lifted her chin up, Lamby recognised that face. Even though he only met her once, he knew the lady right away. Her name was Ida, and she was Charlie's sister who lived in another town. She was sobbing quietly.

Ida peered at Lamby, but looked past the dog. She kneeled down and placed a single, white rose onto the face of the tombstone. Lamby's tail tucked under, and his ears that were usually pricked up and full of personality, now hung down flatly. Lamby gazed down in grief, and Ida looked at him, and her face melted in tears.

"Oh, baby," she sighed, her voice breaking. She lifted Lamby's furry chin to have a good look at him. "I'm so sorry for your loss. I miss him too, Lamby."

Lamby looked up with tired eyes, glassy and wet. Ida rubbed his fur. Tear stains were all over her cheeks. "I just heard the news too, Lamby. He died right near here. On the gold fields. I don't know how though. Oh, baby, you came all this way…"

Ida broke into silent tears, and she wrapped her arms around Lamby's back, who didn't move a muscle. He sat there, letting Ida embrace him. Lamby didn't want to do anything. Perhaps it would be better to just stay here for a while. He couldn't do anything else except sit there and try and feel Charlie's presence.

I didn't even get to say goodbye yet. And you left me. You promised to me that you would come back. Lamby lay his head down to rest.

Chapter Twelve

◆

Pip

"Lamby? Lamby, where are you?"

Pip trudged around, wiping his stained cheek with the back of his hand. He felt terrible for lashing out at Lamby. He was probably sulking somewhere under a bench right now. After all, Lamby was just trying to comfort him. But sometimes you can't push the truth away. Pip sauntered around the street, trying to find that familiar, small dog. But there was no sign.

Pip felt something loom above him. The long shadow cast on top of him, and it seemed to eat him from above.

Pip shifted and looked up. It was a sign that had the words carved into it - *Ashven Cemetery.*

Pip sighed and shook his head. He didn't want to experience anything closely related to grief anymore. However, when he turned to leave, he spotted something on the ground.

Paw prints.

They were most definitely paw prints due to the distinct difference between the colour of the marks and the ground. Though it seemed to be fading, you could make out that the prints belonged to a dog. A small dog. Was it Lamby? Pip couldn't fully guarantee. But it was worth a try to find him.

Pip felt the sudden change in the atmosphere. Why would a dog go into the cemetery by itself? There were no other traces of human footsteps. Well, at least none that were recent. Pip walked down the path of the cemetery. It felt like he was walking through a thick fog and it was too hard to see - who knew what could be hiding. So many tombstones - so many deaths. All crammed into a single place.

Pip looked in the distance, shifting around, trying to find a furry head. He walked around slowly, taking several turns and retreats. There was hardly anyone in the cemetery. Pip bent low and peeked around a tombstone and noticed a furry creature laying in the distance. His eyes lit up for the first time, relieved to find a familiar face. Pip felt a smile tug on the corner of his mouth as he ran closer. And next to the dog was a lady. A lady he didn't recognise.

"Lamby! There you are. Listen, I'm so sorry..." Pip started, but then he started to trail off when he realised that something was definitely wrong.

Instead of wagging his tail when saw Pip, he was coiled up and trembling. His eyes were narrow and dropped, and he didn't dare to look up from the cold ground. Pip frowned and stammered, squatting down to examine the grieving dog.

"What's wrong, Lamby?" Pip whispered, lifting up his head.

Lamby seemed to be glued on the tombstone base, refusing to get up. Pip looked around the area, frantically trying to find the reason why the happy, bubbly dog was now so numb. Pip looked up to the lady. To his surprise, instead of watching Pip break in a sweat, she was sulking tirelessly. She seemed to be grieving over the name of the tombstone.

"What happened? Did you do something to him?" Pip urged demandingly, though his words came out weak and nervous.

The lady sniffed hard. She opened her pursed lips, though nothing came out. "My-my-my- brother. Lam-Lam-Lamby's..." She stopped short and returned to sobbing.

Pip frowned, looking around. "What? Lamby what? How do you know him? What-what seems to be-"

Pip stopped. He looked down at the tiny plaque pressed into the stone.

Charlie Anderson

Pip kneeled down beside Lamby and caressed his soft fur. There was weight over his shoulders. "I'm sorry, Lamby. I never thought that he would have... died. But listen, Lamby. I thought about what you said. How Dennis has a chance of being alive. And you know, we should go and look for him! Come on, Lamby."

Lamby said nothing. He couldn't believe that Pip would switch the topic to himself when Lamby was clearly hurting. He continued to lay emotionlessly on the cold ground, refusing to move. *There's no point now. Charlie's not going to come back. What am I to do?*

Pip bit his lip, unsure what to do. "We came all this way, Lamby. We can't stop now. You always look at the positive side of things. Please. I can't imagine what you're feeling. Losing your owner. Your best friend. A person you've been with all your life. But please. We have to go and try to find Dennis. Perhaps we would run into Charlie too! Maybe he's not dead."

Pip forced a smile, trying to enlighten Lamby. But that just made him even worse.

Pip sighed and looked down. "Please, Beauie. We can't stop now."

Beauie.

Beauie.

Lamby recognised it right away. The nickname. The name that Charlie always used for him. A flood of flashbacks hurled into Lamby's mind but disappeared within seconds. *Charlie.* Lamby looked up, squinting up at Pip which made him pleased.

105

"Beauie! You're really strong, you know? No other dog can do what you're doing. Getting back up after all that," Pip cheered, which made Lamby eventually sit up.

Lamby shook off his tears and licked his lips. Pip was like a mini version of Charlie.

Bye Ida.

Lamby nuzzled the lady's legs, making her smile between tears. She hugged the dog tightly, muttering soft words made to comfort him. Nothing could compare to a dog losing its owner.

Pip led Lamby out the cemetery - away from the misery - away from the suffering. It was time to clear things up. Determination laced Pip's face, which was mixed with hope, fear and doubt. The two walked away from the yard, reaching far away from gloom. There was a chance that someone would recognise the name Dennis Duncan. Pip and Lamby walked to the main entrance of the gold fields, which was surprisingly near the cemetery.

A man in a dark-blue suit walked out of the fenced entrance. He must have been someone working in the gold fields. His face was dusty and black from the dirt he was working with. Pip ran up to him.

"Excuse me, sir. Do you know someone called Dennis Duncan?" Pip said, hopefully.

The man frowned. "Ah, yes. Heard he passed not too long ago."

Pip swallowed bitterly, letting the cold words slam into his face like a wall. "Okay. Thanks."

Pip frowned. That was no help. He looked back to Lamby, who was sitting thoughtfully behind him. Pip shook his head and forced a small smile. But behind the smile was pain.

"Pardon me. Who are you looking for?"

The voice of a man came from behind. Pip hurled around, coming face to face with a young-looking man. He was also wearing similar clothes to the man from before. Pip's eyes widened as he immediately said, "Dennis Duncan. Please, sir, help me. Tell me he's not dead."

There was obvious despair hanging onto Pip's words which made the man straighten up. His ears pricked up, stirred up by the pain in the desperate boy's voice.

"Oh. What's your name?" he said.

"Pip. Pip Duncan. I'm his brother. I came all the way here from Parramatta to find him. Do you recognise him?"

The man hesitated. He looked around like he was unsure what to say. But after everything, there couldn't be anything possibly worse than hearing that Dennis was dead. Pip raised an eyebrow, the fear getting the best of him.

"You're Dennis' brother. He told me about you," the man said eventually. "I know where he is."

Chapter Thirteen

◆

Lamby

Pip's eyes grew wide like dinner plates as he stared at the man in disbelief. Wait—did he hear that right? Did this man know where Dennis might be?

"Where?" Pip blurted out, practically jumping. His voice cracked a little. "Everyone is telling me that he's dead. They say that he fell off while on his journey to the fields. How can I believe you? How do I know you're not messing with me?"

The man cleared his throat and gave a slow shake of his head. "Because I'm a friend of his. And he did go to the gold fields. Well, not necessarily working here, but he came here to ask for directions. We became friends. And he stayed near here for a while. Before... before he told me he was going to leave. He told me that he was planning to board a ship."

Pip frowned. A ship? Since when? And he came to Bathurst but never worked on the gold fields? Pip thought that the only reason Dennis came was to find gold. At least, that's what Aunt Mandy had said... but the truth is, Pip wasn't sure how much of her talk he could trust when it came to Dennis.

"What?" Pip asked, confused and on the edge of ripping off his skin. "A ship to where? And why? Where is the ship docked?"

"I'm not sure where he's going," the man replied quietly, looking down ashamed. Pip's small face faded a light red as he placed his palms over his forehead. Lamby felt tense just by listening to their conversations. "Dennis just told me that he was going on a ship. Nothing else. Not much of a reason either."

"He just left about an hour ago. He went to the dock. But I don't think he's coming back."

"The dock? But the nearest dock is miles away," Pip said brittly.

110

Pip shook his head slowly, and he stared at the ground absently. Confusion and disbelief bubbled furiously in his burning head. What was really going on? First he heard that Dennis was dead. And now this stranger was claiming to be his friend and saying that he was alive and about to go on a ship? Pip squeezed his eyes shut and breathed in. He clenched his jaws tightly. He felt like he was a single, tiny screw trying to hold an entire wall up. The man's lips pressed into a thin line.

"Wait. He told me that the boat leaves at dawn on Wednesday. You can find him. It's not too late," the man assured, but he couldn't even believe himself. "Take a carriage. There's a cab stop just near here."

Chapter Fourteen

◆

Pip

(IN SYDNEY)

The stinging rays of sunlight shone through Pip's eyelids, making him open his eyes reluctantly. His vision was blurred, and it took a second for his eyes to adjust to his surroundings again. He couldn't remember anything that happened. Pip rubbed his eyes and massaged the sides of his face in a circular motion, trying to ignite any memory.

He was on a carriage at the moment to Sydney. He heard that it was a coastal city that was expanding larger at the minute. He was so exhausted that he forgot about what had happened earlier on, before he had boarded a random carriage to a place he had never been to before. A place he had merely heard from people's stories. Large, stretching beaches with golden shores, and those fancy boats moored at the spacious docks.

Pip wondered if anyone even noticed that he was gone. Had any of his classmates realised he hadn't shown up to school? Ben was probably missing his favourite target. And maybe the rest of the class were celebrating that the so-called "teacher's pet" wasn't there to blither on about useless things.

But thinking about it wouldn't change anything. Whether they missed him or not, it didn't matter right now. He had to stay alert and focused in the moment. He had to focus on what was in front of him—because this moment, unlike the ones he left behind, was still his to choose.

The clatter of hooves against the uneven road echoed, growing louder along with the chatter and ship horns. Pip shifted in his seat and leaned forward, pressing his cheeks against the glass window, trying to see past the people and carts.

They were close now. He could tell. The dock wasn't far.

As the view opened up, Pip caught sight of the harbour. Boats and ships were scattered across the water, bobbing gracefully. The water was murky and grey and looked ominous. Some ships were tall and sharp-edged, almost like battleships. Others looked older, with wide sails and peeling paint. There were sleek ones, sturdy ones, and a few that looked like they hadn't moved in years.

And then he saw them—passenger ships. At least four of them, maybe more, all lined up and moored. They were large and chunky, and you could see the top of the passengers' heads. Some of the ships had ramps already down. People coming and going.

Pip's stomach turned. How was he supposed to know which one Dennis was on? They all looked the same from here—just big floating buildings with flags and signs he couldn't read from this far back. Finding the right ship was going to take far longer than he thought.

Then something lit up in the back of his mind. Not all hope was lost - not everyone was a stranger in this situation. He had Grandad Ken. Of course. He worked on the ships here in Sydney. Pip remembered Grandad

Ken telling him that he was the master of boats and ships, and that if Pip ever needed assistance he should find him. If anyone knew where Dennis might be, it'd be him.

Pip sat up straight, his heart thumping quickly in his chest. Maybe he wasn't too late after all. Pip squeezed his eyes shut. Where did Grandad Ken live? Near the docks? Near the markets? Wait. Pip looked up in thought. He traced back to the summer holidays a few years ago, when Grandad Ken visited him and Dennis and Aunt Mandy.

"Oh, I have to leave tonight, Philip," Grandad Ken said, patting Pip's back. "I really wished that you would visit me soon. The beaches in Sydney are beautiful. They have sand as soft as velvet. And it's always sunny. You've been to my house once, when you were two. Do you remember? Near the shore? Isn't it so nice and cosy there? I was pestering your brother to move to Sydney with me."

Pip turned around to the glass window in front. The coachman's rear end could be seen bobbing up and down against the bumpy ground. Pip rolled down the windows and stuck his head out. Lamby stood up, alarmed. Pip felt the hard salty wind blow against his pink face as he peered up at the coachman.

"Sir!" Pip called, gripping onto his little hat for dear life. "Can you drop me off somewhere else? Can you drop me just by the shore? The road down there's fine."

Pip pointed to the road below, at the end of the hill. The coachman looked down to the boy who was barely away from falling onto the road.

"Okay," he said gruffly and tilted his hat. "Sit yourself down, boy! You're going to fall."

Pip swung himself back into the carriage and smoothed down his hair. The carriage turned abruptly, heading down the hillock. Pip stumbled at the turn, crashing to the other side of the carriage. Lamby barked.

"Settle down, Lamby. We're nearly there," Pip said, smiling.

"Sir, you've arrived."

The coachman shifted from his seat and knocked on the glass window. Pip pushed the iron bar on the door and stumbled out. Lamby jumped off after him, shaking his fur and stretching his legs. Pip inhaled deeply, tasting the heavy seasalt and briny air. Today was more of a grey day. Though there weren't too many clouds, the sky was painted a dull, grey-ish blue. The sun was small and pearly, half-hidden behind a wispy cloud. After thanking the coachman, Pip walked off onto the gravel path above the shore. He felt the crunch of rock and seashells beneath his foot as he took each step.

The sky hung low and grey, the clouds smeared across the canvas like ash. Pip stood at the end of the rocky pavement on top of the shore. He watched the rolling waves splutter and cough as they gently swept over the sand. There were no kids on the beach. Only an elderly couple strolling up and down the shores. All the children were at school at the moment. All the children except for Pip. He gazed out to the distance, trying to find the end of the ocean. But the sea, grey and dark, was blended with the sky. Pip imagined the beach to be a sunny, flowery experience. Instead it was a dull, cold one. It was too cold to go in the waves anyways.

Pip jumped down from the rock, and Lamby jumped down after him. The sand was chunky and looked damp, like it had just rained before. Pip waded through the sand, creating dark prints. Little pawprints trailed behind him. Pip staggered around, kicking balls of sand and tangled pieces of seaweed. Then he stopped in his tracks, looking around. He must be able to see a familiar wooden house on the shore somewhere, right? The beach didn't stretch too far. Pip squinted his eyes. Drat. The fog was creeping in. And in not too long he wouldn't be able to see a few yards ahead. Pip groaned and squatted down to the sand in defeat. Lamby whined. The dog trotted around the boy, trying to cheer him up when Lamby noticed something. He kicked the sand, trying to get Pip's attention.

Pip looked up, then to the ground. After a moment of hesitation, Pip's eyes lit up in realisation. There were another set of footprints imprinted in the sand. A rather large pair, looked like one of those men-hiking boots. They were stretched all along the shore, well at least as long as Pip could see. Lamby barked, his tail wagging happily. Pip smiled and patted the grinning dog on the head, and said, "Good job. Thank you."

The two walked off again, following the long trail of footprints. Pip felt lighter now. He really hoped that the footprints belonged to Grandad Ken.

After a few minutes, the footprints faded and led to a set of planked stairs. They were breaking apart and green with moss, and they creaked awfully whenever Pip stepped onto them. Barnacles stuck on the sides of the stairs like tiny houses. Pip's shoulder throbbed in pain - he had been carrying his leather bag for the whole trip. He shifted it to his other shoulder and continued walking.

Finally, the two reached the top of the stairs. The landscape opened up once again - wild grass and brambles laced the side of the land, and low shrubs tangled together at the edge of the sloping cliff. The cliff was empty and open. And then, Pip saw it.

Tucked neatly in the middle of the field - nestled behind a thick bramble - was a small wooden house. Driftwood patched the walls and logs and tarred iron sheets stretched across the roof. The house structure wasn't clean, but it wasn't messy either. None of the logs were sticking out, but pieces of leaves and sticks poked out from the crevices of the planks. A small chimney popped out from the roof, and wisps of smoke drifted out gracefully. Pip stopped. He gazed at the small, cosy hut. It looked like Grandad Ken hadn't moved. Everything looked the same… except that it looked colder and sort of lonely. Perhaps it was just the weather.

Pip crept up to the front porch, his boots crunching softly on the rocks. The hut sat atop a ramshackle platform of stacked stones, weathered and lopsided. The house creaked eerily in the wind, like it was talking to itself in a mutter—old and cranky since it was on the edge of toppling over from the unstable base.

The wooden door was hidden by a sloping awning. A nail was hammered into the wall beside the door. A small, grubby lantern hung under, dust smeared all over the glass. There was one small, round glass window fitted into it, cloudy but barely clear enough to look in. Pip climbed up the cobble steps, trying not to stumble on the slippery moss. He clung onto the glass to look in.

The entrance was dark and still inside. There was a small table in the middle, with a small box and papers scattered across. Pip shifted around, trying to see what was further inside. He could make out half of the kitchen, but it was too dark to see. There were no lit candles or open windows. The only light source seemed to be the round glass on the front door. It looked like there was no one in the house right now.

Pip frowned. He breathed heavily onto the misty glass. Lamby let out a gentle snort behind him, his tail swishing impatiently. Pip looked back and sighed. Where was Grandad Ken? He knew that this was his house. It must be. A few things were different but everything else was the same. Suddenly, the sound of loud clomping thundered in the distance. Lamby looked back, alarmed. And emerging from behind a bush, seemed to be a large, bear-like creature.

Lamby lurched forward and started barking, while Pip, frantic, staggered to the door. The creature, tall and big, slowly made its way closer. But when it lifted its head up, Pip stopped and blankly stared at it, confused. The "bear" wasn't a bear. It was a man dressed in thick layers of fur clothing and a hat. It was Grandad Ken. Pip widened his eyes and his mouth stretched into a large, hopeful smile. He was so happy to finally see a familiar face.

"Grandad Ken!" Pip cried, running past the confused Lamby.

The man's pale face lit up, and he immediately opened his arms wide to embrace the tiny boy. "Philip! What are you doing here?"

"I'm here on a mission. To find Dennis."

"Where's Aunt Mandy?"

"At Parramatta. I came here myself. With Lamby, of course."

Grandad Ken stepped back, confused. He stared at the wagging dog, then to Pip. Did he hear that correctly?

"You came alone?" he asked, his smile fading just a little. "All the way from Parramatta?"

Pip nodded proudly. "I took the coach. I had a sandwich and everything."

Grandad Ken ran a hand through his salt-and-pepper hair and breathed in slowly. "Well… you'd better come inside, then."

Grandad Ken's house was small but definitely not eerie. The house seemed strangely nostalgic, like you'd been inside before. The walls were splashed a warm orange, and the floor was either carpet or oak tiles. The place smelled of fresh peppermint and chestnut, and there was a lingering scent of something toasty - perhaps the burnt out fireplace. The stone fireplace was wide and grey, and it sat in the middle of the wall of the cosy living room. It was like as soon as Grandad Ken entered the house, the whole place lit up with a warm glow. He lit up the hanging lanterns, and the room flickered to life. There were thick blankets and cushions scattered across the saggy couch.

Grandad Ken was a simple and straightforward man. He was much different than Dennis and Mandy, who were often fretting.

"Put your bag down at the bench, Pip," Grandad Ken said, gesturing to the small foot bench in the corner of the entrance. "It's warm in here. Do you need anything? Water? An extra coat? Come down to the living room, I'll get the kettle going."

Grandad Ken switched the brass kettle on and made his way to the small wooden counter. His home felt like those homes in a fairytale. Pip wandered around the living room, running his fingers across the shelf full of ornaments and picture frames. There was a photo of Pip sitting on his mum's lap. He was still small in the photograph. Pip looked at his mum in the photo. She was smiling a small smile and she was peering down at her curious son. Pip gently touched the face of the picture frame. A thick layer of dust coated the picture frame, like it hadn't been touched for a long time. Grandad Ken was probably the only person who had photos of Pip's parents before they passed away.

Lamby looked up at a photograph of Dennis.

"This is my brother," Pip said quietly. He lowered the photograph so Lamby could see properly.

Lamby observed the features of Dennis' face - freckles, faint smile lines, and scruffy hair. He looked exactly like Pip. Except, of course, much more mature. Pip took off his flat cap and showed it to Lamby, who sniffed it. The hat smelled like tobacco and peppermint.

"This hat is my brother's. I often took it from him." A faint smile escaped at the thought of Dennis. "It's a bit big on me."

Pip took out a silver necklace. There were initials on it - KD. They smelt of the same scent as the hat. Tobacco and peppermint.

"This is also my brother's. He wore it for good luck before he passed it down to me. It used to be my great, great grandad's," Pip said, and he bent down and tied the chain around Lamby's neck. "Aunt Mandy says I look handsome in it, but... I think you look better."

Pip giggled and patted the dog's head.

Grandad Ken handed Pip a mug of hot loose-leaf black tea on a small china plate. Pip's stiff, cold fingers immediately softened at the feeling of the warm ceramic mug. Slightly shaking, he lifted the cup to his thin lips and took a small sip. It was the perfect temperature, and it had the right amount of sugar and cream. Just as Pip liked it.

"Scones?"

"I'm in a bit of a rush."

Pip settled down beside Grandad Ken on the couch, who was holding a platter of scones, jam and biscuits. "So, you're looking for Dennis? I heard the news. I'm sorry, Pip."

Pip sipped the tea. "Yeah. But I know where he is. On a ship. And I need your help."

Grandad Ken wiped his beard and raised his eyebrows. "Oh? A ship. Whereabouts?"

"I'm not sure. But he's not coming back. Grandad Ken, do you have any records or history for the passengers boarding the upcoming transport ships?"

Grandad Ken nodded slowly, picking up a scone. He stayed very still, waiting for Pip to say something else, but he didn't. Pip stared back at his Grandad expectantly, a stubborn expression on his face. "Oh. Okay. I'll go take a look."

Grandad Ken rummaged through the files and folders, muttering to himself as he pushed away old maps, receipts and photographs. Clouds of dust puffed up, filling the air. Lamby sneezed from the other side of the room.

"Aha. Found 'em," Grandad Ken exclaimed, coughing a blow of dust as he examined a worn-out leather folder. "These are the most recent ones."

Grandad Ken held the binder like it was an animal and carefully placed it onto the wooden coffee table. It groaned a bit like it refused to be opened. He flipped it open. There were passenger documents, shipping schedules and lots of other folded papers. Grandad Ken pointed at one document. Pip looked over the paper and ran his finger across the listed names. On the top of the page, "*Passengers of The Black Gull*" was printed on. Pip whispered out the tiny columns of names under the title, his eyes skidding across furiously. Then, he stopped at a name and looked pleadingly to Grandad Ken.

"There. Dennis Duncan."

Grandad Ken peered at the name, surprised to find his missing grandson's name. For a moment he thought that Pip was just making things up, like kids do when they don't know anything better. He nodded slowly, rubbing his beard. "Yeah. That's the supply vessel. Transports passengers to the west. These types of transport ships come once a while."

Pip's heart thudded. "When- when will it leave?"

Grandad Ken looked at the date. "If the schedule's right... then at twelve this afternoon."

Pip looked up at his Grandad anxiously. "But that's in less than an hour. Where's the dock?"

"It's further down the coast. Since it's a big ship, it'll need more space." He checked his watch. "We can still make it. On foot it'll take - quickest twenty minutes. It's not too far."

The wind hit them as soon as they stepped outside, slamming into them like a wall. The sky - now dark and threatening - had heavy, black clouds that reflected onto the sea. He followed Grandad Ken down the skinny, winding path that was on the edge of the cliff. There was a large hill that blocked their view of the dock below the cliff. But they knew that it was there. In any moment the ship horn would sound and it would all be over. Seagulls circled above the two, shrieking like vultures.

As they made their way around, the bush began to thin out and their view expanded. The dock was right below the cliff, and there was an enormous ship moored right at the side. The ship was large and sharp, and it was painted dark grey with navy and black stripes. It looked like its name. On the haul, *"Black Gull"* was painted on. At least they now knew what they were looking for. But the hardest part wasn't done yet. There was still a line of boarding passengers, but the queue was shrinking fast.

Pip squinted at the ship. A wave of fear rolled through him, but his legs refused to move. They were glued to the ground, his trembling knees giving out. He felt the sharp, salty wind pierce through him like arrows. Pip stared absently at the ship. Grandad Ken looked at the shaken boy.

"Come on! There's no time. You have to run, Pip," he cried, but Pip just couldn't. His feet were frozen.

A man's voice was hollering below beside the ship. He was wearing a suit, and he walked around the ramp connected to the dock.

"Last call for ship Black Gull - passenger transportation! Last call."

The three looked to the ship. Grandad Ken's eyes grew wide like discs as he looked over to Pip, who was still petrified.

"Pip! Hurry. I understand you're scared but… if you don't start running, we'll miss Dennis! I can't run any further. My legs have given up on me." Grandad Ken pleaded, his voice breaking now.

Pip's pupils dilated as his heart hammered in his chest. His mind flashed. And he remembered Dennis. Dennis probably didn't know what he was doing - getting on a ship and tossing his life away. He needed to be put back into reality. It was now up to Pip and Lamby.

And then, without another word, Pip ran.

Pip sped down the wobbly gravel trail, running faster than he had ever ran. Lamby raced down behind him, soon catching up and then taking the lead. The wind was loud and fierce as it roared past him, slamming into Pip's pink face. Adrenaline rushed through his body, and for a moment Pip couldn't feel fear. Or exhaustion. He felt alive. Soon, Pip made it to the bottom of the large hill. The man in the suit was now pacing up and down, looking for any late passengers. Pip wasn't too far now. The *Black Gull* reflected the murky waters, turning the sea black and thick. It swallowed the space, towering over like a giant. Pip looked up at it, overawed.

Pip muttered to Lamby between huffs. He trudged over to the man in the suit, who blocked Pip's path.

"Sir. Please. I need to get on the ship. Right now," Pip huffed, wiping his forehead. "I need to get someone."

The man looked unamused. "Sorry, kid. Boarding entries are closed."

Pip stuttered. This was not a good time. "My brother's in there. I need to get him out now. It's urgent."

"I already called for last calls. You're too late, I'm afraid. The captain's ready. You can book the next ship at - Hey!"

Before the man could finish his sentence, Lamby swooped between his legs and sped across the ramp and into the ship. Pip's mouth dropped but he quickly closed it. The man stammered and ran into the ship too, chasing after the small dog.

Chapter Fifteen

◆

Lamby

L amby bolted through the doors of the ship, his head
turning in different directions. There were several
doors and hallways and turns. Looking at the size of the
ship, there could be hundreds of rooms. But Lamby just
followed his gut. It was up to him now, to find Dennis.
There was still a chance. He could hear the vague shouting
from the man behind, but adrenaline and determination
blocked his voice out.

Lamby remembered the smell of the hat and Dennis'
face. The dog lifted his wet nose and breathed the sharp

air. There were so many smells. Behind him, the man kept on shrieking. But Lamby didn't care. His nose twitched, breathing in the salts and smells. He made a right. Then a left. Then another left. Lamby could smell the scent of tobacco and peppermint now. It was growing stronger.

Lamby skidded a corner, his paws scrambling against the hard floor. He froze. There was a young man sitting on a chair, his back turned. He was looking out a window. The man had the same scruffy hair. And he had the familiar scent. Lamby stared at the back of the man's head and let out a loud bark.

The man instantly turned around, startled to see a dog standing at the door of the room. He had the same green eyes as Pip, and he had faint smile lines and freckles. It was Dennis. He frowned and stood up slowly, facing the small, unyielding dog. Lamby barked again, his big eyes staring deep into Dennis' eyes.

"What are you doing here, dog?" Dennis asked, bending down a bit. "Are you lost - what - that's my necklace."

Lamby didn't move. Dennis edged closer, his face now stern and confused. Was his mind playing tricks on him? Perhaps he saw it wrong. But Dennis swore that the necklace around the dog's neck was his. Shifting closer, he cautiously untied the chain around the dog's thick fur and put it close to his face. *KD*. That was his necklace. Well, Pip's necklace.

Dennis stared down at the necklace then to the stiff dog. He had never seen the dog in his life - and he has Pip's necklace. This wasn't a coincidence. It couldn't be. Dennis flipped the necklace around. On the back of the initials, there was his great-grandad's full name. It was not a coincidence.

"How did you…" Dennis peered at the small dog, whose tongue was stuck out. "You know Pip?"

Lamby barked once and wagged his tail. Dennis was taken aback. Was this dog a friend of Pip's? Did this dog know what he was doing? Was this a sign? Dennis thought of Pip's grinning face. He thought of him walking Pip to school every morning and him taking him out to the park every Monday evening after school. Dennis couldn't help but smile. What a peculiar little dog.

But before Dennis could speak, heavy footsteps thundered from the hallway. Both he and Lamby looked toward the door. Emerging from behind was the man in the suit. And he looked furious.

"Out!" he shrieked, pointing a trembling finger at Lamby. "Get out, you mutt! Get out of this ship before I do it myself! Stop disturbing the passengers! I'm so sorry, sir, for this disturbance."

Lamby edged towards Dennis. "No need for an apology, sir! And I want to get off the ship. Immediately."

The man stuttered, switching glances at the smug-looking dog and the young man. "Oh! Is there a problem, sir? I'm afraid there's no time, you see, because the ship is about to leave."

"I understand, but I need to get off right now."

Dennis turned around and gathered his luggage. He didn't pack much - just a single suitcase. The man in the suit rubbed his chin as he stood at the door, unsure what to do. The man offered sheepishly to help carry Dennis' luggage but he refused no matter how many times the man insisted. Suddenly, a loud holler sounded. It was so loud that they felt the ground tremble. The horn just went off - that meant that the ship was going to leave. Lamby looked alarmed as he sprawled against the floor.

"We have to go. Now!" Dennis urged, and gripping his suitcase, he ran out the door with Lamby, leaving the embarrassed man alone.

The two sped down the hallways, making several turns and skids. Lamby felt his throat tight and bitter. The air in his lungs felt sharp and stinging. Each hallway looked the same. It looked like they were passing the same places.

They didn't stop.

They couldn't stop.

It felt like they were a second too late. They were nearly at the main entrance of the ship. The ramp was rolling out. Slowly, the ramp retracted from the dock, its metal wheels screeching as it rolled back. There was no more time. Was there? Soon the ramp was fully retracted, and now the ship was slowly moving away from the dock. *No.*

No slowing down.

Don't stop.

There were people blocking their way.
But the two didn't speak.
They just ran.
One last sprint.
Then, they jumped.

Chapter Sixteen

◆

Pip

Where were they? They should be out now. The ship horn had just blared. The ramp was going to retract soon. Pip looked around pleadingly. He felt tears sting. *No.* Did he lose both of his friends? *No.* Pip paced back and forth the dock, hyperventilating. He clenched onto his hair tightly. What if he made the biggest mistake ever? What if he never saw Dennis and Lamby again? Pip's throat felt dry as he rubbed his red, sticky face with his hands.

He heard a shout. A familiar voice. Pip's head shot up, staring at the now leaving ship. And out of the open door, Dennis and Lamby jumped out.

"Dennis?!"

Pip stood up. Was he dreaming? Dennis stumbled onto the dock, sprawling onto the ground. Lamby followed behind, tripping over. Pip ran over to the two, tears streaming down his cheeks as he hugged Dennis tightly.

"Dennis!" Pip sobbed, pressing his cheek against Dennis' shoulder. "You don't know how happy I am. I missed you so, *so* much. First you were missing, then you were on a ship and now you're with me once again."

"You've travelled all the way from Parramatta to here? By yourself and this dog?" Dennis said, dismayed. "Why?"

"To find you. And Charlie. Charlie's Lamby's owner. But he passed in the gold rush."

Dennis bit his lip in guilt. He had let down his loved ones. "Oh. I'm sorry. And I'm sorry, Lamby, for your loss." He was now on the verge of tears after finally seeing his beloved brother. To be honest, he never really knew why he decided to leave his home. Though things were rough, he never really had a proper reason to toss his life away. Dennis sighed and shook his head. "Times just get tough

140

sometimes. But I shouldn't have left. I don't know why I really left in the first place."

Pip peered up at Dennis then buried his face into his chest. "Please don't leave again," Pip said, his voice muffled.

Dennis gave a small smile. "I won't. I promise."

Lamby whimpered quietly, watching the two hug each other. Pip dragged the dog into his embrace and fondled his furry head.

"I knew that the dog was yours. He's a smart one, Pip," Dennis said.

"His name's Lamby. Isn't he cute? I met him at the train station one day when I was at the plaza. And we've been inseparable ever since," Pip said proudly, not looking up from Lamby.

"Aye!"

The three turned their heads. Grandad Ken was walking down the hill, waving a spotted handkerchief in his hand. "Aye! Dennis, is that you?" He squinted his eyes at the three.

Dennis looked up and smiled sheepishly. "Oh. Hi, Grandad. Yeah, I'm here."

Grandad Ken's saggy face was red and ruddy as he looked to Pip then Lamby then to Dennis. "So Pip was right. You did go on a ship. I thought he was just bluffin' at first. But now you've got explaining to do, Dennis. The whole world's lookin' for you. But I'm glad you're safe."

Dennis mouthed 'sorry' as he stood up and brushed his trousers. "Shall we go home?"

"What about Lamby? He has nowhere to go. *Please, please, please* can he come home with us?" Pip begged, not letting go of Lamby.

Dennis looked up, pretending to think. "Well… I always wanted a dog."

Chapter Seventeen

◆

Lamby

The wind was gentle that afternoon, warm and easy as it rolled over the long grass. The air was soft with the lingering scent of wildflowers and sun-warmed soil. It smelt like home.

Lamby lay in the middle of the field on the smooth, warm ground, his little legs tucked beneath him, his eyes half-closed as he embraced the strange but nostalgic feeling. Rolling around him were long, golden stalks, swaying with a hearty rhythm, like they were breathing. A bright blue dragonfly zipped above Lamby, darting in and out of Lamby's view. But he didn't move. He remained still, just watching it, like he had all the time in the world.

Lamby could feel the reflection of the pale blue sky. He was aware of everything around him - a pipit trilling in the large, oak trees, the black ants trailing around him… everything seemed to move slowly. Everything was quiet.

Lamby shifted a bit, letting the golden sun cast its warmth onto the side of his face. He closed his eyes and inhaled deeply. His nose twitched at the faint scent of bark and soil and something sweet - perhaps the aroma of wattle blossoms. Once in a while, a bird would soar over Lamby, its shadow flickering over his scruffy coat. Lamby could hear Pip in the distance, shuffling and wading around the bush in the background. But he didn't bother to get up. He had his whole life to play with Pip.

There was no leash. No collar. Just the empty, blue skies and the stretching gold and green fields. For once, after a long time, Lamby didn't need to worry about waiting for someone to come back.

Footsteps echoed in the background. Lamby slightly opened his eyes. Kneeling in front of him was Pip. Lamby lifted his furry head, one side of his cheek pressed flat due to the straight surface he was lying on. Lamby opened his mouth and let out a long yawn, stretching his paws in front of him. Pip smiled as he twirled his finger through the dog's tangled fur. He bent down and wrapped his arms around Lamby's neck, pressing his cheek onto the top of the dog's furry forehead.

"Lamby. Let's go in for lunch. Aunt Mandy and Dennis are already inside," Pip whispered before he stood, causing Lamby to straighten up.

Pip waded through the thick stalks as Lamby followed behind, prancing over patches of grass. Soon the long weeds suddenly dropped into short, stubby grass. Lamby trotted around the field, his tongue stuck out. He circled around rocks and boulders, his tiny legs working furiously beneath him. He had been living in this cosy little farm long enough to remember the position of each reed of grass, where all the bird nests were and where the flowers bloomed the most in spring. Winter had just rolled past and now spring was creeping in. You could feel the sudden change of temperatures and the atmosphere - an abrupt jump to warmth. Lamby would always choose spring over winter.

Lamby passed the wooden swing, which was installed over a branch of the large Jacaranda tree a few blocks from their farmhouse. The swing was a block of smoothed wood with a fraying rope tied on each corner. The soft breeze made it sway a little. Lamby padded through the moist soil, walking towards a few daisies. He lowered his snout to the flowers and gently plucked the thin stems from the fresh dirt. He held the daisies in his mouth, ensuring that the delicate flowers didn't snap. Pip smiled and giggled. This was their routine, every afternoon before lunch.

Pip plucked a few surrounding daisies and placed them onto his palm. He coiled them and twisted them, curling and weaving, making a daisy chain. Drool dribbled from Lamby's chin. This was Lamby's favourite time of the day. Probably better than dinner time.

The two trailed around the swing, heading towards the cobblestone slabs that led to an elevated stone floor. The round platform was decorated with a curved flower bed made to fit the shape of the edges, and it looked like a short flower barrier wrapping around like walls. And in the centre of the platform was a beautiful rosebush with four tall roses thriving out. The petals were a majestic red, soft and velvety, with dewdrops hanging on the leaves. The soft aroma of rose and fresh rain contaminated the area, like a sign that you were about to enter a special zone.

At the root of the bush was a bronze plaque, along with a small, grainy photograph. The plague was embedded in the stone, and it read *Charlie Anderson*. Comforting words were printed under the bolded name. Lamby gazed at the small square, staring deep into the name. But instead of feeling the gloomy, sad feeling he felt the first time he saw his owner's grave, he felt unusually peaceful. Like he knew that Charlie was in a safe place now.

The photograph had Charlie's face on it, and even though his lips were pressed, you could tell that there was a smile bubbling behind his still face. Four rocks were pressing the photo down. Lamby kept his stare, something hopeful fizzing inside of him. An abrupt breeze brushed past Lamby's fur. It felt as if Charlie was with him at the moment, sitting on the steps, wandering out into the distance. It felt sweet just by thinking of Charlie.

Pip stood behind him. Lamby looked behind and nuzzled Pip. He smiled, and patted the grinning dog. The daisies were drooped in Lamby's mouth. Lamby bent low and gently placed the daisies onto the feet of the rosebush. Nothing happened. Just peace. Pip pulled the daisy chain off his wrist, which was wrapped around like a loose elastic band, and he placed it onto the top of the photograph. The daisy chain flopped languidly onto Charlie's head in the photo, covering his eyes a bit. Pip smiled and Lamby shifted closer to Pip's side.

Then he saw him.

Charlie. Now standing behind the platform, emerging from behind a rose. He was grinning a big grin and he stretched his arms out welcoming. And there was a daisy chain weaved on his head. Lamby's eyes lit up like stars. The stars dropped into tears. Happy tears. They rolled down the side of his cheek as he barked and stood up abruptly. But somehow, he was stuck to the ground. He couldn't move. He kept barking, hoping Charlie would come closer. But he didn't. He couldn't. He just stood there, his arms spread and his beam bigger than ever.

Charlie! Charlie! I missed you! Oh, you're finally here. I have so much to tell you. I'm so glad you're back!

"Oh, Beauie, I missed you too! You have grown a lot! And you've got a new friend, I see. I cannot stay for long, however. But we will meet again soon."

No, Charlie! Please don't leave again! I've got a new family and so much has happened since you were gone.

"I'm sorry. I love you, Beauie."

No, Charlie! Don't go. I went to Bathurst to find you but instead I...

Charlie?

Lamby stared out. *Charlie?* He came back so easily. As easy as he disappeared. Like sand flying in the wind. Lamby knew Charlie wasn't going to come back in a while. But a visit was nice.

Pip stepped back. Lamby gazed down at the photograph. The flowers. They sat so perfect and imperfectly on his head. Lamby smiled.

Flowers look good on you.

www.ingramcontent.com/pod-product-compliance
Lightning Source LLC
LaVergne TN
LVHW091301080426
835510LV00007B/347